"The best of the fu

BUCK CREEK

True Stories to Tickle Your Mind

DR. JERRY PATTENGALE

*All proceeds from the first printing of this book were donated to
The Community School of the Arts*

www.csa-marion.com

© 2013 by Dr. Jerry Pattengale

© 2013 DustJacket Press
Buck Creek: True Stories to Tickle Your Mind / Dr. Jerry Pattengale

ISBN: 978-1-937602-73-4

All rights reserved. No part of this book may be reproduced or transmitted in any form or by any means, electronic or mechanical, including photocopying and recording, or by any information storage and retrieval system, without permission in writing from the publisher.

Dust Jacket Press
PO Box 721243
Oklahoma City, OK 73172

www.DustJacket.com
Info@DustJacket.com

If you purchased this book without a cover, you should be aware that this book is stolen property. It was reported as "unsold" or "destroyed" to the publisher, and neither the author nor the publisher has received any payment for this "stripped book."

All Scripture quotations, unless otherwise indicated, are taken from the HOLY BIBLE, NEW INTERNATIONAL VERSION®. Copyright © 1973, 1978, 1984 by the International Bible Society. Used by permission of Zondervan. All rights reserved.

Cover and Interior Design by D.E. West
Stock Images: Deposit Photos

Printed in the United States of America

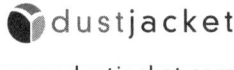

www.dustjacket.com

This book is dedicated to my cousin, Danny Pattengale, one of my favorite people—and the only person I know who has ridden a wild deer down the freeway, against traffic.

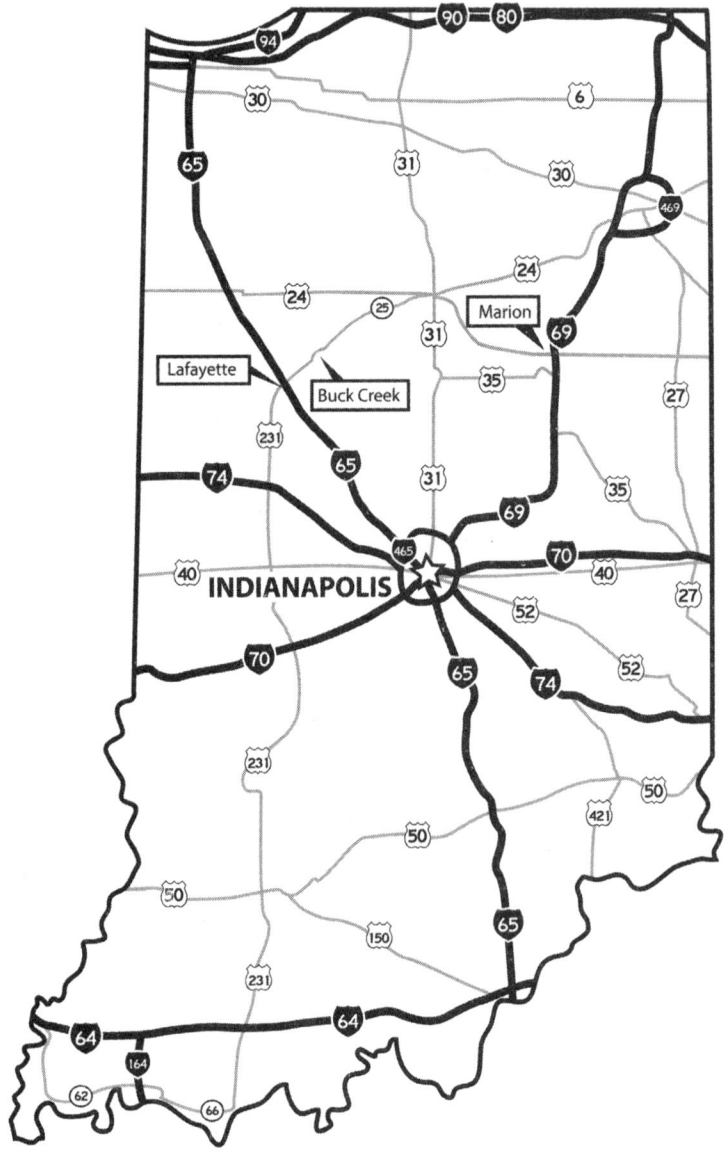

The true stories in this book take place in or around Buck Creek, Indiana. Today, the author lives in Marion where he serves at Indiana Wesleyan University.

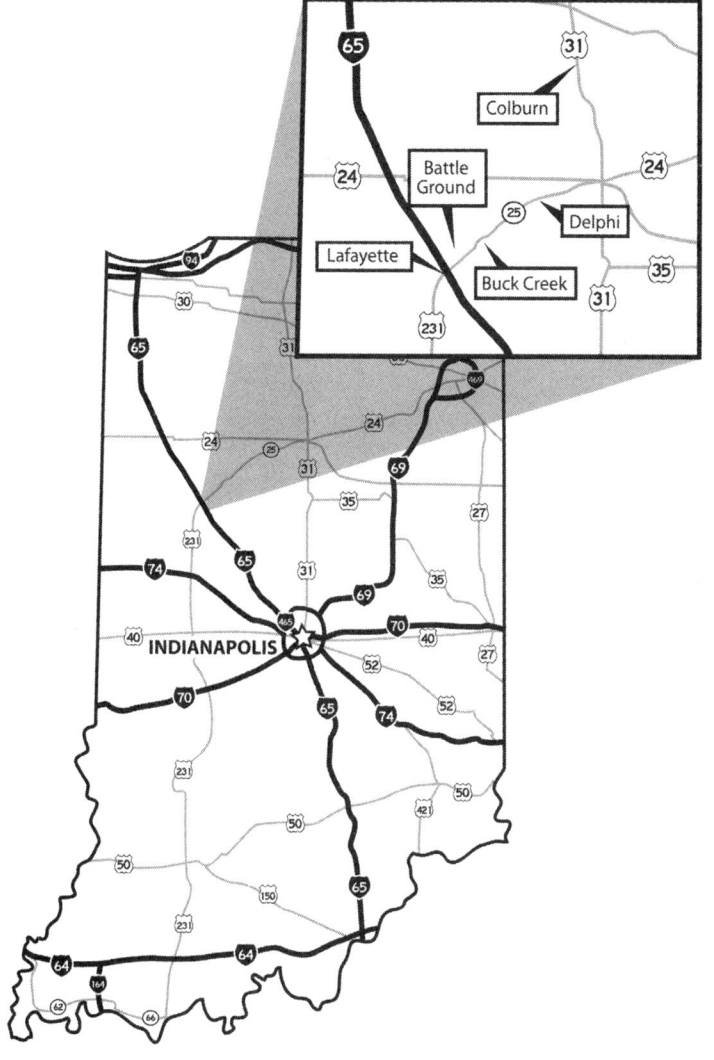

The author lived much of his childhood in the woods just north of Buck Creek. In these stories, "Buck Creek" refers to his stomping grounds which included the towns marked.

Table of Contents:

Introduction — xiii

Chapter One:
Forced to Face the Naked Truth — 1

Chapter Two:
It's Not Just the Size of the Man in the Fight — 5

Chapter Three:
Snaking Our Way Through Poverty — 11

Chapter Four:
Throwing Apples Can Have Consequences — 15

Chapter Five:
Platform Shoes and Baggy Pants — 19

Chapter Six:
Shooting for the Right Goals — 23

Chapter Seven:
Playboy in the Pigpen — 27

Chapter Eight:
Make Room for Other People's Crises — 31

Chapter Nine:
Making the Most of the Moment When it Hits — 35

Chapter Ten:
The Men in Black — 41

Chapter Eleven:
An Afro at the Crossroads — 45

Chapter Twelve:
Throwing Away Prize Possessions — 51

Chapter Thirteen:
Falling on a Deer Ruins the Surprise — 57

Chapter Fourteen:
Buck Creek English and Life Rhythms — 61

Chapter Fifteen:
The Buck Creek Diet — 65

Chapter Sixteen:
Buck Creek Track — 69

Chapter Seventeen:
Christmas in Buck Creek, Indiana — 73
Chapter Eighteen:
Don't Surprise Your Wife with an Ab Blaster — 77
Chapter Nineteen:
Deer on the Freeway — 81
Chapter Twenty:
Dead Priests and Alive Issues — 85
Chapter Twenty-One:
Hunting Deer with a Musket — 91
Chapter Twenty-Two:
Reality TV Super-Sized Me — 95
Chapter Twenty-Three:
My Neighbor Punched James Dean — 99
Chapter Twenty-Four:
I Wore a Scarlet Letter to College — 105
Chapter Twenty-Five:
Pigs on Roof: A Buck Creek Reflection on Faith-Based Initiatives — 109
Chapter Twenty-Six:
Dynamite and Explosive Ideologies — 113
Chapter Twenty-Seven:
When Old Women Speak - The Easter Chicken — 119
Chapter Twenty-Eight:
Bad Hair Day: When Your Wig Falls Off in Junior High — 123
Chapter Twenty-Nine:
Driving in Circles — 127
Chapter Thirty:
Buck Creek Golf — 131
Chapter Thirty-One:
The Poster Girls of Buck Creek: Natural Beauty and Mature Eyes — 137
Chapter Thirty-Two:
Losing Your Marbles — 141
Chapter Thirty-Three:
Shooting Grandma on July Fourth — 147

Chapter Thirty-Four:
Bottoms Up in Buck Creek 153
Chapter Thirty-Five:
I Didn't See a Corvair at the White House 157
Chapter Thirty-Six:
Waking Up with the Answers 161
Chapter Thirty-Seven:
Stealing Pop and Smashing Pears 165
Chapter Thirty-Eight:
Swimming the Wrong Race 169
Chapter Thirty-Nine:
Worms in Square Knots at Blue Heron Lake 173
Chapter Forty:
Fast and Furious: Wrong Turns with No Return 177
Chapter Forty-One:
The Lesson of Red Ryders 181
Chapter Forty-Two:
No More Tiptoeing through Human Trafficking 185
Chapter Forty-Three:
Waving at Ayn Rand with Tube Socks on Your Hands 189
Chapter Forty-Four:
Naked Ned and Catastrophes 193

About the Author 199

Dr. Jerry Pattengale

INTRODUCTION:

Buck Creek is a real place, and the following stories are true.

Some of the accounts are indeed bizarre. It's not every day one sees a man riding a deer down the freeway, an 80-year old woman serving ice cream naked, or pigs piled on a car roof. Other stories strike at our common temptations and challenges. Finding a *Playboy* in a pigpen or having your girlfriend's wig fall off could happen to anyone—or at least experiences of private choices, discoveries and embarrassment.

While psychologists have many terms for these behaviors, in Buck Creek we simply call them "life."

PBS filmed me in Buck Creek for its special, *Leading the Way out of Poverty*. During that event, I began to see anew the role my eventful childhood had in preparing me to lead. And though some herald me as successful and have bestowed honors, the truth is that I often pinch myself to make sure I'm not dreaming. I've enjoyed a wonderful and rich life, but never consider myself far from Buck Creek.

I'm embarrassed to admit that for twenty years I didn't write about my childhood; I desired space between my career path and my impoverished past. But thank God I found myself, though the journey to authenticity was a long one. It's a journey that continues for all of us. If you try to make an impression, that's the impression you'll make. I have long since tried to be nothing more than a guy from the backwoods who benefited immensely from education and faith. And, one who discovered that "the dream needs to be stronger than the struggle." That's my mantra.

I was 40 years old and flat bellied when I began writing these stories known to my newsprint readers as "The Buck Creek Chronicles" written by the "Accidental Author." I'm now 54, and my boys tell me in an XL T-shirt I look like a shrink-wrapped pear. But I'm happy. The widespread response to these articles confirmed that simple can be significant, self-effacement can be endearing, and perhaps more importantly that most people relate to struggles; and on a lighter note, that we can all kid about interaction with relatives and lifelong friends. The joy of knowing that each week people would begin their Tuesday with a Buck Creek insight has indeed been fulfilling. Buck Creek goes to press in book form, *Buck Creek* the series continues in the *Marion Chronicle Tribune*. This is the first book of several, for which I'm thankful.

So you see—Buck Creek is a dozen years in the making. I've started and finished other books during this time, but this one couldn't be rushed. Like the neighborhoods that read the newsprint stories through the years, I hope that through these reflections you can begin many days in Buck Creek as well.

Buck Creek is a little shadow of a town several miles from any highway, just northeast of Lafayette, Indiana. During my childhood, it bustled with life on a limited scale: a blacksmith, several homespun businesses, and a stalwart brick school atop a grassy knoll. The railroad track still frames Main Street, but except for the weathered grain elevator, it's a sleepy town with a handful of nondescript houses, a traditional-spired church, Euchre parties, and veteran flags.

We lived back in the adjacent woods, driving through Sugar Creek to reach our makeshift home (since collapsed). No sidewalks. Only a partial flat roof. No indoor plumbing during our first year. Old stock cars spread throughout the woods. A few pigs. Dogs and unnamed cats. A lone cow. Tall grass. Snakes. Raccoons. Deer. Raspberry patches. More snakes. Rhubarb clumps. Mushrooms on hot spring days.

The episodes you're about to read aren't just funny or engaging stories; rather, they're platforms for life success principles. You might say it's the Buck Creek way. Many readers haven taken treks to Buck Creek to visualize some of these stories. Some have sent postcards, letters and emails reflecting on their pilgrimage.

Perhaps this book will prompt you to take trips to your own past in order to visualize your future. In the meantime, laugh and cry with me as I've expended over a decade to frame a few episodes to enrich your journey.

As you'll discover, Buck Creek was not without its bumps. Indeed, "The dream needs to be stronger than the struggle." Oftentimes, looking back helps stepping forward, regardless of what's ahead.

And if you find yourself at the book's end curious about Buck Creek, a new highway is cutting through this sleepy area that will afford you easy access. I suppose for a few more years you'll be able to catch a glimpse of the people and places that surface in the pages ahead. After that, Buck Creek will follow the fate of nearby Battle Ground. Executives from Lafayette, Indianapolis and Delphi will likely discover its majesty, give it a makeover, and project it into a somewhat more picturesque future.

CHAPTER ONE:
Forced to Face the Naked Truth

She answered the door naked. It was an awkward moment for my youngest brother and me. She was over 80. We had come to mow our new neighbor's yard, but that didn't seem important to her just then. Instead, she thrust open the door, grabbed my arm, and pulled me inside. My brother, affixed to my other arm like a parasite, followed suit.

She directed us to sit on the couch, and still in shock, we obeyed. When she disappeared into the other room, my brother pressed his hand tightly against his baby-toothed grin and tried to control his giggles. I offered a kick in the shin to help him.

When she returned, she placed two bowls of ice cream in front of us then sat down across the room to pull on her stockings. The plain vanilla scoops were a welcome relief from the awkwardness, and I focused intently on eating that ice cream slower than I had ever eaten anything before. Still, out of the corner of my eye, I caught her performing a sort of geriatric hop as she navigated her way into her girdle.

She disappeared several times more, returning each time with a new piece of clothing. While she buttoned, we nibbled on tiny spoonsful trying to make the ice cream last until she was fully clothed.

Finally dressed in a mismatched outfit and sporting a disoriented wig, she sat between us on the couch and guided us through an album of old photographs. The 80-year-old woman sitting next to us was nowhere to be found; instead were black-and-white snapshots of a gorgeous woman, flanked by business executives, and dressed in wools, silks, and other exotic materials completely foreign to two cotton-clad boys from Buck Creek. If not for the matching gap between her front teeth, I would never have guessed that the goddess in those pictures and the loose-skinned lady hobbling around that musty house were the same person.

When she opened the door, I wanted to run away from the woman who was our new neighbor, but when she cracked that photo album, I wanted to know the woman who inhabited those pictures—the successful world traveler, the stately career woman, the well-kept woman with the porcelain skin. Where had she gone? It was as if she had taken life's bus from the center of the world to the farthest reaches of oblivion, where she'd become our neighbor.

Today, years later, I still think about that lawn-mowing job. I sometimes ask myself, "Decades down the road, will I answer the door naked?" "Will young neighbor kids not yet born find me delusional?" and "Will I one day be a stranger in my own land?" The most-pressing question the episode prompts is: "Am I striving for goals today that I'll discover matter little when I reach life's twilight?"

That twilight may come at 99, as it did for my great grandmother, or it may come "mid-life," as it did for my father. Though most of us would prefer a long life, Catherine Marshall offers a valuable perspective on longevity in her book, *A Man Called Peter*. It's about her husband Peter Marshall, the U.S. Senate Chaplain who passed too soon. She writes, "It's not one's duration in life that matters, it's one's donation."

Lisa Beamer, wife of Todd Beamer, one of the heroes of Sept. 11, reflects on her husband's early passing in her book *Let's Roll*. She relates that on his office inbox, Todd had taped the well-known quote from Theodore Roosevelt: "The credit belongs to the man who is actually in the arena . . . Who strives valiantly, who knows the great enthusiasms, the great devotions, and spends himself in worthy causes. Who, at best, knows the triumph of high achievement and who, at worst, if he fails, fails while daring greatly so that his place shall never be with those cold and timid souls who know neither victory nor defeat." His duration in life was far too brief, but he put himself in the arena, and his donation was enormous.

I occasionally read Martin Luther King's "I've Been to the Mountaintop" speech, which he delivered the evening before his assassination. After expressing gratitude for great civil rights gains, he said, "Well, I don't know what will happen now. We've got some difficult days ahead. But it doesn't matter with me now. Because I've been to the mountaintop. And I don't mind. Like anybody, I would like to live a long life. Longevity has its place. But I'm not concerned about that now . . ."

From Marshall and Roosevelt to King and Beamer, and from our aging neighbors, we learn that we should give first-rate priorities to first-rate causes. One day, whether we're giving our last address to a Senate floor, staring down a terrorist, delivering our own 'Mountaintop' speech, or dipping ice cream naked, we'll have expended our life's best energies.

We'll all look back at life's photos and either smile or glance away. My neighbor saw something in her pictures that framed her life's fulfillment. That gaze in her eyes erupted into a smile—a beacon of pride.

In retrospect, I witnessed a royal moment. In our youth, we're distracted by nakedness, however innocent. As we mature, we should be more preoccupied with the naked truth, whatever it may reveal.

I received a flood of comments after a version of this story appeared in the *Chicago Tribune* (on March 4, 2003). I wish I had space to share all of the hilarious stories—and also the touching memories. One of the funniest calls I received was from a dear friend, Katie Beaver, the 90-year old matriarch of our church whose husband served as its first pastor. She stood around five-feet tall, with a baritone laugh that would fill any room. Katie announced on the phone: "Jerry, this is Katie. I read your article." She paused and I began to sweat. Then she blurted, "Just wanted to let you know I still have my clothes on! . . . Gotcha!" Then she burst into laughter.

But she also paused again to say thanks, and reflected a bit on her own personal journey. When she passed away a few years later, all who knew her knew she had lived a full and rich life.

BUCK CREEK: *True Stories to Tickle Your Mind*

Buck Creek Wisdom #1

All quotes in these wisdom sections are mine, unless otherwise attributed.

"Give first-rate priorities to first-rate causes."

"The dream needs to be stronger than the struggle."

"One day, whether we're giving our last address to a Senate floor, staring down a terrorist, delivering our own "Mountaintop" speech, or dipping ice cream naked, we'll have expended our life's best energies."

Buck Creek & the Bible

Jesus spoke to religious leaders of his day about abundant life. In the following passage, he is sharing against the backdrop of a shepherd and his flock. In this analogy, he is talking about his role on earth as the "Good Shepherd" and protecting the sheep, or people—and in a sense, you and me. "I am come that they might have life, and that they might have it more abundantly." (John 10:10)

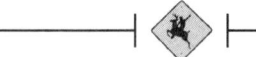

Dr. Jerry Pattengale

CHAPTER TWO:
It's Not Just the Size of the Man in the Fight

When Rick's leg fell off, the schoolyard fight took a sudden turn. When his eye popped out, winning was out of sight.

Momentum built all afternoon at our junior high school. That old brick school was abuzz about "the big fight."

Steely-eyed, Rick was around 6'3" with one real knee, and he challenged a heavyweight wrestling star with twice the girth. Big Bob's comment about Rick's limp was the last straw.

The fight commenced as both opponents rounded the grassy circle exchanging ferocious punches while the crowd swelled.

Then Big Bob did the unthinkable—he dove for the prosthetic leg. It was rumored to be stainless steel with riveted skull and crossbones. It was allegedly a weaponry appendage.

From the testosterone-laden dual flew a simple, outdated, shiny, caramel-colored leg. Nothing more.

Rick was poor. All the more reason to cheer for him.

The crowd passed the leg back Rick's way.

Preoccupied, he tossed it aside.

Big Bob charged again.

Rick bobbled.

5

Time stood still.

With a collision as certain as Andy Kaufman and Chuck Liddell, facial disaster loomed. Bob launched a George Foreman swing that was two counties wide and packed two weeks of hurt. With Shrek-like arms and wrists like rolled doormats, he introduced Rick's head to the laws of physics.

Thud! Like a dropped bag of seed on a tilled garden, it left a predictable impression.

Silence. Panic. Stares.

Rick's eyeball was on his cheekbone! Pandemonium ensued.

"Help!" came from the crowd. "Someone help! His eyeball! Look at his eyeball! Oh my! His #%&@ eyeball!"

Like Monty Python's dismembered Black Knight, Rick would have fought to the end. But this wasn't a movie scene; it was painfully real and bizarrely surreal. Finally, a teacher arrived.

It was time for Rick to pull himself together, literally.

A large gawking crowd watched a dismantled, proud, young teen deal with what we called a handicap, reattaching his leg to an abbreviated femur while a teacher held his eye in place.

Big Bob won a Pyrrhic victory: he won the fight, but Rick won our hearts and respect.

Rick had fought for his dignity. Big Bob had pounded into him the truth that life's challenges are no respecters of personal challenges.

But Rick inflicted upon Bob the reality that a person's response to and through challenges establishes respect.

Although the days of defending one's honor with a schoolyard fistfight are over, maintaining honor through challenges is not.

Competing with challenges will always remain honorable, whether in life issues, such as Rick's defense of dignity, or in athletic and vocational pursuits.

The Tour de France reminds the world about overcoming challenges through challenges is not without temptations for shortcuts. Thousands still wear yellow rubber Livestrong wristbands—a play on the name of Lance Armstrong. His well-publicized recovery from cancer was a motivating story in the light of his cycling accomplishments. However, the glory proved ephemeral when his illegal drug use earned him a life ban from the sport. Just competing at a top level drug-free would have been an amazing accomplishment.

A lesser-known story played out in Grant County, the area including where we live in Marion, Indiana (an hour east of Buck Creek). The captain of Lakeview High School's baseball team battled Crohn's disease and was sidelined for his senior season.

This once muscular player—our oldest son—had lost thirty pounds and most of his energy.

He learned to navigate daily a blender of pills, surgery, emergency room runs, Prednisone, and regular Remicade treatments.

The day finally came when Jason went from his occasional chair near the end of the dugout bench to a chance at bat. This former standout had a batting average of .000 entering the last game.

He unexpectedly received a chance to bat against a friendly rival, the Mississinewa Indians.

From my Denver hotel room, I listened to my wife's play-by-play description.

The crowd was still yelling for Jason. In the quiet of my room, uncontrollable, happy tears flowed near the Rockies. We had no warning that he might play, so it was all the more joyful.

But just as quickly, Jason was off the bases, picked off trying to steal second.

I hung up, thanking God that Jason, though no longer an all-star, was able to see his star shine again before hanging up his cleats for good.

That final high school season was filled with prayer. That he could walk normally. That tubes would be removed. That major surgery could be delayed or avoided. That he could at least sit in the dugout for home games.

Now, I thanked God repeatedly for that hit.

It was a legitimate hit. The pitcher didn't sit down. The catcher didn't hesitate. The umpire didn't fudge the calls to help a sick kid.

Like most of life, it was played out by rules not adjusted for Jason's challenge. And Jason's play became larger than life.

But that's the key: it *was* life. In all of its fullness. With a challenge. With a champion. Regardless of the score.

Kneeling beside my bed, I began to lose it. I couldn't see straight. I couldn't pray straight. I kept envisioning Jason with his raised arms and magnetic smile. I couldn't string sentences together.

The phone rang. Cindy was calling again.

"We won! We won! Joshua [our second son] hit a double to the center field fence. We won! We won! Can you believe it? Jerry, we won!"

Lakeview had not beaten a larger county team for many years.

That season ended. One son, the captain, had one hit. The other led the county in batting. We rejoiced with both.

One's personal challenges don't lessen another's accomplishment. Likewise, one's accomplishment doesn't nullify another's fulfillment.

That's a life lesson—facing the same challenge, regardless of personal challenges.

Life is full of surprises and sudden turns. Jason managed to do back flips for the nationally ranked cheer squad at Indiana Wesleyan University in between handfuls of pills and treatments. Oh, he missed a game or two, but he's not missing life's fullness. These days, after having his colon removed, he's back to a rather healthy life—and his first job after college was taking care of others! He's fully aware that the dream needs to be stronger than the struggle.

It shouldn't take a prosthetic leg flying past us to become sensitive to another's challenge. We should appreciate people's fight to survive, to live fully with dignity, regardless of challenges and gifts.

Buck Creek Wisdom #2

"It's not just the size of the man in the fight; It's the size of the fight in the man"

"One's personal challenges don't lessen another's accomplishment. Likewise, one's accomplishment doesn't nullify another's fulfillment."

"Challenges perceived as boundaries limit the likelihood of crossing them."

Buck Creek & the Bible

The Apostle Paul wrote much of the New Testament, and the following carries much authority given his personal journey. He had endured considerable hardships from physical abuse and ridicule to imprisonment and also worked throughout his ministry to pay for his own expenses: "I can do all this through him [Jesus] who gives me strength." (Philippians 4:13)

CHAPTER THREE:
Snaking Our Way Through Poverty

When the four-foot-long snake dropped in front of me, my shower was over.

It's one thing to run into your living room screaming. It's quite another to do it naked.

I sounded like a high-pitched rap-off between Drew Carey and P. Diddy with a touch of Willy Nelson, and more obvious than Kanye West at a Taylor Swift concert.

I had just noticed the snake above me in the unfinished rafters when it began to lower itself.

It was surrealistic—a snake, me with no fig leaves, and I wasn't in Eden.

As I looked for my towel—thud!

Silent screams. Frozen reaction. Just me and the snake.

My dad had finally begun to add an indoor bathroom to our Buck Creek home, nestled near the bank of a hill with underground springs.

Our Spartan flat-roofed house was on a floodplain with Sugar Creek snaking through our land. It was wet, overgrown property frequented by an assortment of reptiles. But until that moment, they were always *outside* the house.

Although the plumbing worked, I could still see the sky through the quasi-permanent plastic roof sagging from puddles of rain.

Dad was at his usual watering hole. Nine of us remained at home with no phone or car, left to devise a snake removal plan.

"Maybe music would hypnotize it like the cobra on *Johnny Quest.*"

"Let's put a trail of bread crumbs."

If snakes knew English, this one would be having a hissing fit of laughter.

As the oldest son—all of twelve years old—it fell to me to be the leader.

Finally dressed in my briefs and surrounded by four hysterical sisters and three younger brothers, who considered me some sort of divine snake conqueror, I took action.

Crammed in the unfinished doorway, my sibling audience watched as I drew my bow. The hunt was on.

Razor-sharp arrows do serious damage to an uncovered plywood floor and unpainted sheetrock. They didn't damage the snake at all. I would have had to hit the thing.

Eventually, I resorted to stabbing it with the arrow.

Finally, I became a snake-conquering hero—Buck Creek's Asclepius. In reality, my mother actually finished it off.

For her, it was yet another episode in her impoverished life of bad but almost unavoidable situations.

She weathered numerous house moves, cold and drafty winters, an absent husband, and no social life. Finally, we had found cheap Indiana land, and it was our chance to have our own home.

Beautiful land, but in a floodplain. Land susceptible to acts of God out of our control.

We had to drive *through* Sugar Creek to get to our house. The only bridge was our headlight beams.

On occasion, the current pushed our dated station wagon downstream. Mom screamed as Dad calmly set aside his brown, long-necked Falls City, opened the door and began carrying us to shore.

When the creek rose, Dad parked along the gravel road and loaded us a couple at a time into a rowboat. He had fixed a cable across the creek about shoulder high and used his hands to pull us to the other shore.

During every trip, Mom would cry from shore. Though unchurched and non-religious, she would pray aloud with eyes wide open. Her prayers were laced with expletives about Dad. Some troubled waters need to pass before returning home.

For sixteen thousand dollars on a land contract, we managed to buy fourteen acres of throwaway land.

In the end, though, the water dampened our hope to end our string of rentals.

The house no longer stands, thanks to the elements. We eventually lost the land, and, in time, the marriage that had weathered many storms faced one too many.

With each anniversary of the 175-mile winds of Hurricane Katrina and the HBO *Treme* series, we wade anew through water, still crossing rough emotional and financial seas.

For many, the impoverished in the Big Easy had limited options. No cars. No plane tickets. Few relatives outside of the area.

It's easy from a northern Starbucks to ask, "Why didn't they leave?"

But for many, it was a risk to leave work and known support.

For others, it was their real or perceived lack of mobility.

My mother had no phone or car and eight kids for whom to care. Her choices were few, but her fortitude high. Eventually, when the waters subsided she did leave both the land and my father. But she found more thorns in the path ahead.

Through the years, churches provided help and support, and all these decades later, we've all survived.

We need to realize that "acts of God" shouldn't be limited to unavoidable insurance catastrophes.

"Acts of God" also are associated with miraculous recoveries, remarkable lives of character and purpose formed during crisis.

Amid news of American criminals, Afghani snipers and Iraqi bombers, there remains a pervasive knowledge of goodness among humans—the "oughtness" that C. S. Lewis says guides us to do good.

People along the Gulf Coast realize that snakes in their homes are symptoms of a larger problem—in this case, much bigger than themselves.

Our hope is that marching from areas of crisis is a host of children destined to be leaders, fixed on making a difference in such situations and realizing that millions of good people are reaching out.

The next time a snake drops in front of you, remember that it may be a symptom of a larger problem. But as with our Gulf Coast compatriots, such knowledge doesn't negate the immediate danger.

Buck Creek Wisdom #3

"The only bridge to some shores may be our own headlights."

"Mobility is a criterion for security but doesn't guarantee it."

"Poverty often limits options, but the most impoverished are those not considering change."

"Some troubled waters need to pass before building a bridge home."

Buck Creek & the Bible

King David reflects on God's provisions, showing both the struggles of leading a people and his awareness of the countryside from his days as a shepherd, "The Lord is my shepherd, I lack nothing. He makes me lie down in green pastures, he leads me beside quiet waters, he refreshes my soul. He guides me along the right paths for his name's sake. Even though I walk through the darkest valley, I will fear no evil, for you are with me; your rod and your staff, they comfort me. You prepare a table before me in the presence of my enemies. You anoint my head with oil; my cup overflows. Surely your goodness and love will follow me all the days of my life, and I will dwell in the house of the Lord forever." (Psalm 23)

CHAPTER FOUR:
Throwing Apples Can Have Consequences

I didn't mean to kill my Uncle Buck's giant pig.

The Buck Creek school bus occasionally dropped me off at Buck's neighbors, my grandparents.

Buck's house was tucked between several of my relatives' on Railroad Lane. More than one hundred fighting roosters dotted his grassless yard.

My grandparents begrudgingly awakened daily to this strutting symphony.

Throw in a few pedigree hound dogs, an occasional deer carcass strung from the tree, car parts, black plastic flapping on the roof, red sandy shingle siding in disarray and mounds of firewood—and you have one disgruntled grandma.

My handsome uncle was the consummate hunter—and one of the cleanest.

One night after coon hunting, Buck fell through his shower floor. He found a scrap of plywood, jerry-rigged it back together using a long-handled car jack for support—and finished his shower.

When his house burned, firemen had to climb over a stack of antlers in the living room. After living in a hand-painted aqua camper by the river, he managed to put a modular where his old house stood—but the adapted foundation was backwards. The front door faced the back yard, and my cool cousin Danny's bedroom window, which isn't so cool.

My adolescent logic in helping my grandparents deal with their menacing neighbor was disoriented.

Buck was raising two monstrous pigs: would-be hoofed trophies for the county fair.

If he hadn't lived in town, such a quest would have been fine. But two half-ton porkers a few yards from grandma's kitchen window were too much.

The boar was disgusting, even for farm lovers. The worthless, male wallower looked like he was sporting basketballs between his legs, and grandpa had to explain such a phenomenon to his dozens of grandchildren.

Another uncle (only two years my elder) had a plan to teach Uncle Buck a lesson. He recruited a towheaded third grader—me—to help sabotage the "largest pig" effort.

He learned that mustard caused severe diarrhea in pigs. So, we bored giant apples and filled one with mustard. When that ran out, we filled the other with horseradish. We plugged the tops and then heaved them into the lot.

The plan began to go awry when the boar snagged both stealth laxatives.

We waited. Nothing happened to the pig.

However, we almost wet our pants in anticipation.

The next day after school, a funny white truck with side boxes was at Uncle Buck's. Grandma called me to her house immediately and ordered me to stay in the yard. The big boar was acting strangely. The "veterinarian" was out.

I hid near the fence for a long time. The shrillest of moans from the boar informed me that the horseradish and mustard must have worked.

I surmised that the hog had lost considerable weight and that by the time he mended, it would be too late for the nearing contest. A Grinch-ish smile curled there behind the tall-grassed fencerow.

The vet began warning Uncle Buck that he should protect the sow from the same mysterious fate. I couldn't make out all the words through the squalling moans.

The vet took something out of his truck.

Then, "Boom!"

Time stood still. No more piercing sounds. Silence.

No more pig. I saw the two shake hands, and the white paddy wagon left the roughshod dead-end lane.

God suddenly seemed real—the purveyor of judgment. Guilt ripped through me. Many weeks passed before I asked to visit my grandparents again.

I wished against reality that I could take back those apples and somehow relive that day.

There have been a few apples heaved over fences since then, and I continue to learn.

Fortunately, none of my gaffs have been as unforgiving as seeing that dead mountain of pork and dozens of deranged fighting roosters fluttering in fear.

However, from time to time I hear verbal apples tossed over sacred fences of dignity and integrity.

"Hymie town."

"I did not inhale."

The breeding of athletes.

"Look at that monkey run!"

"I am not a crook."

"I invented the Internet."

The endorsement of Thurmond's 1948 platform.

Once those apples were launched, the consequences were no longer the sender's to decide—regardless of the intention.

My days since Buck Creek have also taught me not to give up hope.

After decades of tolerating selfish bizarre life choices, my ninety-year-old grandparents came to find Uncle Buck a perfect neighbor.

Their view began to change when Buck's wife took ill with cancer.

"He never left her side. There 'til the end."

The waning years of her hard burdensome life were transforming. Deep within her scheming husband was a sense of decency and responsibility hidden for decades.

If you drive down Railroad Lane, you'll find retired, robust-chested roosters, caged bloodhounds, a labyrinth of so-called collectibles and a backward modular. Not all has changed.

But you'll also find a freshly showered cigar-smoking Buck caring for his elderly neighbors.

We should be hesitant to write off those who have thrown apples over sacred fences, or those who have established their own fences of insensibility. We should also learn that the divine attributes not only include judgment, but also mercy and grace.

Buck Creek Wisdom #4

"The intention of an action is often disconnected from the consequence."

"Be hesitant to write off those who have thrown apples over sacred fences, or those who have established their own fences of insensibility."

"The divine attributes not only include judgment, but also mercy and grace."

"Before you put a pig out of its misery, be sure the misery isn't yours."

Buck Creek & the Bible

The speech that Jesus gave to his disciples as the crowd gathered near the Sea of Galilee is commonly referred to as "The Sermon on the Mount." It begins with the "Be-Attitudes," and three of them are especially relevant to this chapter. "Blessed are the merciful: for they shall obtain mercy. Blessed are the pure in heart: for they shall see God. Blessed are the peacemakers: for they shall be called the children of God." (Matthew 5: 7-9)

CHAPTER FIVE:
Platform Shoes and Baggy Pants

My introduction in 1973 to platform shoes was a total of ten steps and a turned ankle. The swelling looked liked a softball in my sock; I was four inches taller but with a pronounced limp. On my skinny legs, my shoes looked like twin Rhode Islands on sticks.

The inaugural fashion show was indeed entertaining for my poor neighborhood. To make matters worse I also had flared cuffed pants with a pattern common to picnic tables and a matching jacket with a six-inch elastic waistband. You could have stretched it between two trees and launched water balloons the size of garbage bags.

Yeah, a Woody Allen caption would have read, "Look at me, I'm wanting your attention!" Or, "Don't put potato salad on me, I'm not a table." I would have been too loud even for an Austin Powers film or the Jackson 5's debut. My inflated self came crashing down, literally, when I caught my right heel in my left cuff atop the steps in the old brick school. While I'm sure those pants ballooned like a parachute, the fall was hard and my pride was in worse shape than my sense of style. It's one thing to be poor with dignity; it's another thing to be poor and realize you've just spent your hard earned money on stupidity.

It was a rainy day, and the initial fall had soiled my knee. On the long walk home, my cuff dragged in the mud and my shaggy hair looked like a wet Afghan hound. At least I could limp through mud puddles without getting wet.

I rarely wore those clothes again. My thick adolescent ego realized that my Motown attire awakened the sleepy farming community of Buck Creek, Indiana. Even Motown would have labeled me "Super Freak," and it wouldn't have been a compliment.

It's funny. In the late '70s, I had all that extra elastic in my waistbands, and today's "pants on the ground" boys have none.

A few years ago, a student from Rochester, New York arrived on our Indiana college campus and looked about as out of place as John Madden in Pacemate cheerleading clothes. He sported a tall, spiked Mohawk, and its color varied. His clothes were all variations of black, vintage Gothic, and he had metal studding everywhere. His six-foot-four frame accented his accents. In rural America he might as well have carried a sign – "I know I scare you, so just leave me alone." He eventually met a girl cut from a similar cloth, lip-ringed and carefree. Nearly a decade later, they're married and our family friends—great folks with bright futures.

Rob is now as bald as a cue ball and jokingly considers it divine punishment for his radical hair days. I don't recall any outward radicalness in either him or Rebecca, now a smart-looking but casual couple. But there remains a radical fiber in them that I hope never changes. Just as I had stepped way out in my picnic pants and platforms, they had in their Gothic look. Their tinge of radicalness is attractive, a desire not to follow status quo but to excel in whatever they do—whether in investments or social work—one feeding possibilities in the other. Or spending an extended time helping kids in Romania. Or buying up a city block in Indianapolis. Or forgoing TVs for the sake of focus. Or doing without furniture. Or not eating out.

You get the picture.

Rob played in a somewhat disoriented, ill-prepared heavy metal band during his senior year. It was a low-key battle of the bands, and his group was pitiful. His partner's outfit was especially hideous. And, quite frankly, I think they forgot the words to every song. But I wouldn't have missed it for the world. In that moment, Rob celebrated life in its fullness. Years earlier, he had weathered an extremely tough childhood in a rather oppressive city. His punk look frightened would-be attackers. On our campus stage for fifteen minutes, he simply gushed with life. While the dissonant music pierced my aging ears, my heart smiled. It was, indeed, the most authentic band of the night. No prizes flying their way, but these otherwise good musicians were simply having fun. They made noise, not music, but had within them music that would one day make some pretty important noise in this world.

In recent years, some of my students appeared to be from wealthy homes, but I learned that their parents were either unemployed or working new jobs in rather demeaning roles. Conversely, one student looked like he crawled from beneath a rock but was rather blessed with parental support—and had his act together. A few seemed rather simple, until their blogs revealed strokes of brilliance and a depth considerably deeper than my picnic pants years. One student dressed in drag—but seemed bright and full of life. A decade later, he occasionally stays in our family's guest room.

Yeah, I suppose I'll always want to strap a bungee cord to the belt loops of the low riding rapper pants, take a lawn mower to hideous hair, and throw rubber bands around elephant pants—but I'll also want to reach and respect the core of these same students, to help them to ask and address life's ultimate questions that will long outlive any fashion either of us endure.

Buck Creek Wisdom #5

"If you try to make an impression, that's the impression you'll make."

"When people perform bad music loudly, they're likely screaming unscripted lyrics."

"Today's fashions are rarely worth tomorrow's sacrifices."

Buck Creek & the Bible

The Old and New Testaments have many statements against egotism and selfishness. When we think of Christian examples commonly endorsed by the masses, like St. Francis, Mother Teresa, Pope John Paul III or Rev. Billy Graham, the pervasive characteristic is humility. The following is one of dozens of passages that could be shared on this subject: "Live in harmony with one another. Do not be proud, but be willing to associate with people of low position [or willing to do menial work]. Do not be conceited." (Romans 12: 16)

CHAPTER SIX:
Shooting for the Right Goals

As I swished my long jump shot, the packed gym roared. Suddenly, I was very alone. They were the wrong fans, and that was the wrong basket.

There was nowhere to hide.

In the celebrated Indiana state basketball tournament, I had earned legendary status in an instant, for all the wrong reasons. My team lost. I retired as a freshman.

Throughout my Buck Creek youth, I pretended to hit the winning shot—to reenact Rick Mount's corner fade-away buzzer-beater against Marquette. To dribble like Billy Keller, glide like Oscar Robinson, spin like Pistol Pete.

I hit the long jumper at the buzzer. I basked in the applause. For a few euphoric moments, I lived a dream.

For a lifetime, I've relived the nightmare.

With a few seconds left, the coach inserted two new players.

They immediately ran to the wrong basket and yelled, "We're open!"

As the shooting guard, I shot. The only consolation, in retrospect, is that there was no three-point line.

During the throbbing noise of laughing, foreign fans somehow became muted. An out-of-body experience ensued.

I wanted to pull my knee-high, gold-striped tube socks over my shaggy head and disappear. All three of us—the majority of our team—had run to the wrong end. I had taken the shot.

I spent a decade on the court that day. It seemed never ending.

The consolation game was miserable. Throwing up was always an option.

Every defensive rebound brought chants of "Shoot!"

It's a disheartening feeling to discover you've shot at the wrong goal.

While speaking at various national educational conferences, I discovered many well-meaning educators running in the wrong direction.

Unlike my rogue jump shot, their efforts are not all for naught—but with consequences.

In an effort to help students succeed—to graduate—many college programs are not focused on motivating students but on moving them through the system.

I surveyed educators from over 400 institutions and discovered their programs focused on addressing student dissatisfaction. Many colleges survey students and determine what is most important to them and in what areas they're most satisfied or dissatisfied.

The co-developer of one of these surveys, the Student Satisfaction Inventory (SSI), was co-editor of my book—*Visible Solutions for Invisible Students* (USC, 2000).

It's helpful and necessary to have a pulse on student perceptions. The SSI's theory seems logical: Determine what students deem as most important, ascertain which of those areas are the most dissatisfying, and then address those areas in an effort to retain students.

In other words, goes the theory: happy customers are more likely to stay—to graduate.

This approach may be helpful in determining student perceptions, but it's inherently flawed in helping educators to help students succeed.

I've postulated in other writings that colleges have established an office of "Student Non-Dissatisfaction" instead of "Student Success."

Fredrick Herzberg's research shows that removing dissatisfaction does not mean that one is satisfied and that areas of dissatisfaction have little to do with true motivation.

The movie *Stand and Deliver* aptly illustrates true student success. Jamie Escalante's urban Hispanic students excelled amidst numerous dissatisfactions in an abysmal Los Angeles educational situation. They committed to a cause and were motivated to succeed. He addressed what educators call the student core.

He shot at the right basket while the majority of his colleagues screamed from the other end. Students are capable and deserving of learning noble causes and their underpinning values.

It's usually easier to see the game from the bleachers, and it's obvious when a bushy-haired high-socked shooter and his teammates are off course. But in the fast pace of the game, standing amidst the court's rapid decisions, it can get confusing.

While having dinner at the Escalante's Pasadena home, I was again reminded of his success at student success. Domino-like stacks of award plaques were in the garage and others in the living room corner. Few were mounted.

Jamie understood the applause. It wasn't about him, but *them*, and pursuing the right goals.

While the majority of his colleagues yelled for him to get with the program, he stayed focused on a different goal—true student success and not student non-dissatisfaction.

Buck Creek Wisdom #6

"It's disheartening to learn you've shot at the wrong goal, and devastating to learn you succeeded."

"Removing dissatisfaction doesn't lead to satisfaction, only non-dissatisfaction."

"The sidelines are for perspective not performance."

Buck Creek & the Bible

"For I know the plans I have for you," declares the Lord, "plans to prosper you and not to harm you, plans to give you hope and a future." (Jeremiah 29: 9-10)

Dr. Jerry Pattengale

CHAPTER SEVEN:
Playboy in the Pigpen

I found a dirty magazine in a pigpen. I didn't know whether to shout "Halleluiah!" or look for a lightning rod. While sows were rooting near the backside of the shed, I thought God was about to strike me dead.

The sight of a bare belly photo on the hog house floor introduced me to adulthood's door. I was there to repair the building but found myself in a fix. Like the recent golden treasure found in the British farmer's field, I had stumbled onto a collectable gem. But instead of dealing with Anglo-Saxon luster, it was polychromic lust.

Though not a church-going boy, I somehow associated that 1950s *Playboy* with seedy pleasure and divine retribution. Certainly, I was on the threshold of death or some gnarly wart-covered plague. Already sweating from my summer job, now I was drowning.

A partial *Playboy* among pigs and out of sight from humans—what was this junior-high boy to do? "Mama said there'll be days like this, days like this, there'll be days like this mama said." Days when temptation would come knocking—and it found me, of all places, in the recesses of a mediocre non-descript farm near Buck Creek, Indiana.

Surrealistic? You bet.

There I was on all fours with my bottom still sticking out the door, frozen with eyes fixed on the floor. No swine flu, just swine poo. The half-exposed, pig-trampled and mud-riddled model caught my boyish curiosity.

The faint rumble of an *Allis Chalmers* tractor seemed a fitting backdrop as my own motor began to run.

Not due at the farmhouse until supper, the only thing between me and a May West look-alike was my conscience. In the end, I had the Swiss cheese restraint of Jerry Springer. I began to explore a new world from the recesses of a disheveled shelter. Through the light of the doorway and near the shadow of a hairy boar, I looked through that photographic window into Hugh Heffner's world.

Each page carried the weight of Dante's leaded robes, and each glance zapped considerable mental energy and left images stretching for weeks. The eyes of my Marty Feldman curiosity took over. Instead of stepping through the wardrobe and meeting Girbius and Tumnus in Narnia, my doorway led to life-size bunnies from Chicago.

Although the women were clothed in Wonder-Woman-type garments, it became a time of passage for my virgin eyes. I spent a month in that sweltering pigsty that afternoon. I began to wonder if the pigs somehow knew what was going on, if those lipless grins masked their souls. Perhaps they were Baptist pigs, and I'd need to dip in the trough to cleanse my conscience. Or, Catholic sows demanding a mud genuflect. Maybe they were the Rev. Crenflo Dollar type demanding a monetary penance. But I was sure they were the Hawthorne type, and I'd have a scarlet letter emblazoned on my chest—a "P", and it wouldn't be for Puritan.

Then it happened. Unlike Herbert, the novice treasure hunter uncovering the Anglo-Saxon golden gems, I also discovered the treasure's owner. My evidence was archeologically tight, it was *in situ* (in situation)—exactly where it was left! Near the tattered glossy lust guide was the wallet of the farmer's son!

A couple years earlier, he had advertised widely of his billfold loss. Like the eye of Mordor or Big Brother's one-way mirror, actions seem to make their way back to their maker.

Suffice it to say, supper wasn't my most prudent moment.

In a smoke-filled room of farmers jabbering across mounds of fried chicken, buttered bread and cheap coffee, I nonchalantly informed the group of the wallet discovery. The farmer's son bolted from his seat yelling—"That must be the one I lost! Where'd you find it? Should have around eighty bucks in it!" I pulled it out, and at twelve years old, I knew I had center stage.

"Yeah, that's my wallet—and the money's still there! Thanks! Here's twenty. . . Where'd you find it?"

"In the far hog house, next to a *Playboy!*"

Well, suffice it to say I'm lucky to still be alive. Although most of us didn't go to church, the farmers' wives did, and my older teen neighbor just lost face to a once innocent, freckled farm boy he had picked on for years.

As we look at today's leaders, we're not surprised that wallets are being left behind—and less than noble actions revealed. The measure of a leader is what is done when alone, and manifests in what's done in public. In my neighbor's case, he expended undue energies trying to find his lost wallet—forgetting about his lustful excursion, not to mention the money spent on his vice. Life energies and resources flittered away.

Whether it's ACORN or Enron, onlookers tend to stumble on or seek out lost wallets. Sometimes, a novice treasure hunter will find a treasure, and the discovery will reflect brightly on the deceased. And other times, like professionals digging into ACORN's past, a one million dollar cover-up for a brother and a viral tape of a pseudo-prostitute surface. We find truth pieces we wish weren't part of life's puzzle.

ACORN's humble, Arkansas origins and inherently good charter resonates with my sensibilities. But recent discoveries about sordid political fertilization reveal that a misplaced acorn can produce some unwanted branches.

Yeah, I was innocent when I crawled through that hog house door, but not when I left. Innocence waned when surprise turned to ponder; curiosity melted into complicity. And just like that naïve twelve-year-old, we often make discoveries that demand decisions, and either by design or default we make them—learning as much about others as ourselves.

Buck Creek Wisdom #7

"Lustful decisions often have an unwanted longevity."

"The measure of a leader is what is done when alone, and such character usually manifests itself in what's done in public."

"We often make discoveries that demand decisions, and either by design or default we make them. Leaders rarely rely on default options."

"Like the eye of Tolkien's Mordor or the Orwellian Big Brother's one-way mirror, actions seem to make their way back to their maker."

Buck Creek & the Bible

While being questioned about his teaching and actions, Jesus reminds his accusers that his life was not kept secret, and implies he had not been hypocritical. "I have spoken openly to the world," Jesus replied. "I always taught in synagogues or at the temple, where all the Jews come together. I said nothing in secret." (John 18:20) We are also cautioned against being an actor or *hypocrite*: "How can you say to your brother, 'Brother, let me take the speck out of your eye,' when you yourself fail to see the plank in your own eye? You hypocrite, first take the plank out of your eye, and then you will see clearly to remove the speck from your brother's eye." (Matthew 7:5 and Luke 6:42)

CHAPTER EIGHT:
Make Room for Other People's Crises

My sister asked me the oddest question as the school bus arrived. "Jerry Allen, where are your pants?"

"Oh, my!" I dropped down and tried pulling my corduroy coat with fake fur fringes to my knees.

No wardrobe malfunction. I plain forgot.

I stood out like a black polar bear on a snowy Indiana field.

No, it was worse, like a Dukakis Democrat at a Rush Limbaugh welcome-back reception.

The snub-nosed bus rolled up to our remote country lane with half-frosted windows full of expressive faces. I had reached the bus winded from the long run, but in my long johns.

Boots, thermal socks, mittens, books, sack lunch, and an Elmer Fudd hat, and stark white thermal underwear never intended as a Buck Creek fashion, especially for an undersized sixth-grader trying to appear normal.

I might as well have worn a neon nametag flashing "Abby Normal."

Somewhere in the rush of the morning, I forgot to put on my trousers.

School days were routine.

Cheerios with two spoons of sugar. Milk from our uncle's cow. A quick look at Willie McCovey and other baseball cards. A jaunt down to the pigpen for chores. Then, back to grab my books and bag lunch before running to the bus, trying to beat my sisters after their five-minute head start.

That was my routine. Predictable. Perfectly timed. Personally productive.

We lived down a quarter-mile lane, deep in the woods and out of sight from the world. Only family members saw me run out for chores in long johns. But this morning, I tarried a bit too long.

If you listed one thousand items never to forget before catching a school bus in Buck Creek, pants would be number one every time.

The bus driver looked at me as my sisters disappeared up the steps and into the gawking crowd. The friendly but blunt driver leaned on his wheel and asked a simple but revealing question, "Well little guy, what's it gonna be?"

I was a squirrelly twelve-year-old before fifty laughing peers, and all he could ask was "What's it gonna be?"

I thought he was kidding.

My choices were further humiliation or forfeit my perfect attendance. If I had a snow shovel, I would have dug a hole and hibernated until adulthood.

On awards day, my name was not called.

I needed help, but the driver had his route in mind, no wavering.

"What's it gonna be?" not "That's okay, take my coat." Or, "Hey kids, I want you all to close your eyes." Something. Some help.

But "What's it gonna be?" was all.

He smiled, shook his head, and reached for the metal lever. He was off on his route and his routine.

The bus door closed, and I stood half-clothed in the shape of a question mark, looking straight ahead. Sunken shoulders. No eye contact. I pretended to read the bus letters as they passed by, and I figured my life was over as I once knew it.

And for awhile, it was.

I finally looked to my right to see the back bus windows crowded with hysterical Hoosiers.

The long walk back home was lonely and cold. I wished for the daily routine.

It wouldn't be the last time I longed for routines, wishing for those simple days of predictable schedules and friendly faces.

But I would begin to notice when one person's broken routine called for adjustments in those of others.

This was never more pronounced than while in Washington, D.C. as I walked near the 14th Street Bridge over the Potomac River, the site of the horrific Air Florida 90 plane crash, January 13, 1982.

That day, 80 people aboard a 737 routine flight were confronted with an interruption—a concrete bridge.

Ice build-up, usually detected during routine checks, caused the crash that left only six passengers still alive in the frigid Potomac, amid fierce winds.

The banks immediately became covered with onlookers, but nobody knew what to do.

Suddenly, Lenny Skutnik, a young office assistant from a government agency, jumped in and saved a woman from certain death.

Soon, other rescuers joined. It was a heroic effort of a quiet, behind-the-scenes civil servant who had been about his daily schedule.

As I approached the sight in 1985, I asked the hotdog vendor near the bridge if he had been there that day.

"Yes, oh, yes," he said. "I'll never forget that one."

I pushed for more. "Were you one who jumped into the water? That was a remarkable sight."

"*#$% no! Young man, I got a pint and went home. That was too much for me to handle. People screaming. Lights everywhere. It was one crazy afternoon, and the traffic was clear down that road!"

In a sense, he asked himself, "What's it gonna be?"

His daily routine didn't allow for others' crises. Some routines, like the vendor's, are self-serving. Others bring security to self and others.

When interruptions occur, we need to ask ourselves, "What's it gonna be?" Then add, "You or me?"

Some routines protect the greater good and others ensure personal gain.

Perhaps it's time to establish new routes that veer from our secure paths to those in disarray, where thousands have seen their routine trips to work slammed against closures.

During these tough economic times, some are sinking. No matter how well those on the banks articulate a plan, sooner or later, we'll need to get our feet wet to help the unfortunate.

Yes, we need routines that help us to reach our destinations, but we also need to help others to reach theirs.

"What's it gonna be?"

Buck Creek Wisdom #8

"No matter how well we articulate a plan from the banks, we usually need to get our feet wet."

"True character stands the test of time, and especially through untimely interruptions."

"We need routines that help us to reach our destinations while helping others to take steps toward theirs."

Buck Creek & the Bible

Jesus reminds us often of the value of all life, that every person has dignity. In what has become labeled as "The Golden Rule," he emphasizes the value of considering our own treatment while interacting with others: "So in everything, do to others what you would have them do to you, for this sums up the Law and the Prophets." (Matthew 7:12)

CHAPTER NINE:
Making the Most of the Moment When it Hits

You've never stared ugly in the face until a catfish big enough to swallow your head is about to do so. Lean forward and listen in as I recount one of my more bizarre Buck Creek adventures. Monday recesses were often brag sessions about weekend fishing, and on this particular day, my story reigned supreme.

My uncles took me noodlin' on the Wabash. In drab homemade flat-bottom boats, we headed down river. With a lantern dangling from a makeshift holder, we edged along about twenty yards from shore.

My role was to stand on the plywood bow with a gig—a six-foot pole capped with a miniature pitchfork. We were after blue bellies.

These enormous "bank cats" had heads more than two-feet wide. Beady eyes located near lethal stingers. Bodies ranged from three to five feet long. Their weight was substantial enough to bulge the neck veins in two grown men trying to push them into a boat.

Uncle Bill walked along the banks feeling for prey. The ogress fish backed into holes, allowing Bill's hand to find their flat, ugly lips. With his pinky and index fingers extended and the two middle fingers folded back against the palm, Bill would fool the catfish into thinking his fingers were worms—or noodles.

My great grandfather's noodlin' story was reminder enough of the dangers involved. His father's friend was tired of the big ones getting away, so he hired the blacksmith to rig a large hook that fastened around his wrist—against numerous warnings.

"Beneath Lafayette's Brown Street Bridge," mused my ninety-two-year-old grandpa, "the fella, hooked into one, went under—and we never saw him again." Such stories added to the suspense of standing on a plywood boat with a makeshift spear.

That night on the Wabash with my uncles, the tension mounted whenever Bill paused and dipped low into the water, sometimes submerging part of his head. Slowly, cautiously, he reached into the unknown muddy recesses and into the slothful jaws of an unsuspecting monster.

The water was especially calm. Time stood still as we waited, at times holding our breath, watching.

Suddenly, water exploded. Bill jumped back. His hand was hurt.

"Son of a...! It's a giant! A giant, Jerry Allen! Get it!"

The Orcan mass came directly towards the lantern and suddenly lurked beneath me. The water magnified its appearance to whalish proportions. I had seen big fish—ones filling horse tanks in local bait shops—but never this size.

The ruckus unsteadied the boat. My gig somehow missed the enlarged target, and the throw sent me tumbling near the shark-like dorsal fin. In an instant, my life flashed before me.

Instead of Jonah and the whale, it was going to be Jerry and the catfish. In those few seconds, the largest fish any of us had ever seen excited and eluded us. In a flash, the biggest prize was gone.

My friends had seen big cats and scarred hands. The story had credibility. It had adventure.

Clueless about noodlin' being illegal, my third-grade buddies began scheming for a chance at the legendary fish.

Such opportunities are rare. Oh, we caught some amazing fish in the years ahead. My grandfather landed a record Spoonbill catfish—twenty-six pounds of ugly. I caught an eighteen-inch smallmouth bass in Sugar Creek on a generic Zebco 202. But the Lock Ness blue belly still swims free.

In some ways, that night on the Wabash became a reference for all other fishing trips. It was a defining moment. It came so quickly, so unexpectedly—even with all the folklore and preparation.

Looking back through the years, other moments have defined more important issues for me, and concomitantly for our town and country. Each nation could say the same.

For the Scotts, William Wallace's speech at the Battle of Sterling Bridge reigns supreme, defining its country's patriotism. The movie *Braveheart* covers the 1297 event, and offers the following dialogue as the Scots were outnumbered three to one:

WILLIAM (in front of his troops): "I am William Wallace, and I see a whole army of my countrymen here in defiance of tyranny. You have come to fight as free men, and free men you are. What will you do with that freedom? Will you fight?"

VETERAN SOLDIER (to William): "Fight against that [3-to-1 odds]? No, we will run, and we will live."

WILLIAM (in reply): "Aye, fight and you may die; run and you'll live. At least a while." (Shouting to all now.) "And dying in your beds many years from now, would you be willing to trade all the days from this day to that for one chance, just one chance to come back here and tell our enemies that they may take our lives, but they'll never take our freedom?! Alba gu brath! [Scotland forever!]"

Another defining moment occurred in 1775, in the shadow of the Old North Church. Although they accomplished other noble deeds, for Paul Revere and Robert Newman (who hung the lanterns), the midnight ride became a defining moment, immortalized by Longfellow's poem and the nation's survival.

For the New York firefighters and police, September 11 brought such a rare moment. All the training, heroic Monday discussions and anticipation hit in an instance.

Perhaps some lost their balance. Some may have missed the target. But we have enough evidence to celebrate an overwhelming heroic response.

The same is true of the Texan stand at the Alamo, the Jews at Masada, the Spartans at Thermopylae and the Allies at Normandy—all heroic struggles against overwhelming odds. When the waters gushed and the monstrous moment presented itself, defining moments occurred.

In each case, crisis bred clarity. In a sense, the decisions were made long before the defining moment. History records their actions and their actions inspired a people.

While noodlin', one uncle stood on the back of another to keep him under long enough to grab the fish. Before doing so, he asked the rod-less angler, "If I'm standing on your back, how will I know when you've got a fish?"

Flipping away his filterless Camel and grinning, he replied, "Oh, you'll know."

And, he did.

You'll know when a defining moment hits. What you learn is up to you, and what you contribute defines you.

Buck Creek Wisdom #9

"It helps to put words to your defining moments before the mundane blurs their meaning."

"Time only stands still when our minds capture it, and we're mindful to do so."

"We're responsible and culpable for what we put our hands on, even when we don't initially understand what we've grasped."

Buck Creek & the Bible

In the Old Testament book of Ecclesiastes, we find a chapter reminding us that "Of making many books there is no end, and much study wearies the body." (12: 12) The emphasis is on keeping the Bible as the main focus of our study, especially in the light of the proliferation of secondary works. The latter works might be enriching, but they are indeed additional teachings. This verse is often quoted out of context, or at the least without reference to the chapter's thesis found in its opening line: "Remember your Creator in the days of your youth, before the days of trouble come . . ." The chapter ends with "Fear God and keep his commandments, for this is the duty of all mankind. For God will bring every deed into judgment, including every hidden thing, whether it is good or evil." (Ecclesiastes 12: 13-14) These "Buck Creek and the Bible" sections are inserted with an eye to this reminder. That is, while the Buck Creek stories may often bring laughter while emphasizing a moral, this "deed" of writing them stems from a direct reliance on deeper biblical truths. The laughter from my anecdotal stories is ephemeral, but the joy of their foundational truth is eternal.

Dr. Jerry Pattengale

CHAPTER TEN:
The Men in Black

I looked around at a group of men wearing plain, black suits, Buddy Holly glasses and retreaded wing tips. I had been duped—this "men's meeting" wasn't a breakfast. Instead, it was a 7:00 a.m. prayer meeting with a bunch of "holiness" preachers.

We were at a large ultra-conservative family camp in Frankfort, Indiana. The whole whitewashed building affair was new for me—and one I nearly missed.

My jacked-up, souped-up, black Gremlin drove onto that campground and might as well have been a deer with a target for a birthmark. When I stepped out wearing a tank top, shorts, and sporting a hairdo that was a cross between a mullet and a shag, the camp elders asked me to leave. I was a longhaired, high school kid in a funny looking car with extra-wide chrome wheels, and, according to the preacher-turned-security-guard, likely only interested in the girls.

Well, he was right about the last part.

I knew a couple of them and noticed something was different from other girls at school—wholesomeness. Couldn't articulate it, but could spot it. They didn't smoke pot, weren't running with loose

41

guys and were generally polite. And, some of my guy friends were there, like Phil. Although he had tricked me into going to that men's meeting, he was also among the group who caught me as I was pulling away from the camp. They convinced me to stay and informed the temporary parish police patrol that I wasn't a criminal. My friends loaned me shirts with sleeves and long pants, and "camping" was on.

However, Phil wasted no time in pulling a fast one on me. He knew I'd be out of place with the camp elders at the men's meeting. He couldn't resist himself. He also pulled one of the funnier things I've seen in a religious service.

We were all asked to kneel at the altar at the front of the expansive, simple, studded tabernacle (somewhat of a sacred barn). Surrounded by Johnny-Cash-appareled preachers, I stayed quiet and hoped it would all pass quickly. As a non-Christian from Buck Creek, which I didn't think was even marked on God's map, prayer was a bit outside my comfort zone.

Then it began. The consensus leader, a deep-voiced man, asked, "Brother Smith, will you lead us to the throne of grace?" I couldn't help but think—What's that? Who is Grace? Where's the throne? The only thrones in Buck Creek had flush handles on their porcelain backs.

In unison, the dark-cloaked group removed their hats and knelt on the cement floor around simple wooden altars that seemed to stretch to eternity. Brother Smith began in a thunderous voice, "Dear Heavenly Father, we beseech you…"

Way down to my left a voice joined in—while Brother Smith was still praying, "Oh, yes-a Lord-a…!" A third one piped in, "Oh, ah, Lord-a…" Before I knew it, I was in a room of chanting Charismatics at sunrise. That large, nearly empty tabernacle was full of loud voices.

"Yes, ah, Lord-a!"

"Oh, ah, Lord-a!"

"Thank ya, Lord-a!"

And then Phil, quiet until this point, blurted out:

"Sold-a, to the man in blue-a!"

Time stood still. My heart raced. I'm sure they thought that the longhaired transplant, me, not the shorthaired choirboy, Phil, had played the auctioneer.

That was a memorable first encounter with leaders in a branch of Protestantism known for its conservative doctrines. When the consensus leader (called District Superintendent, DS, or Brother Batman) began to pray aloud, somehow the rest of them knew to stop. With his final "Amen," the meeting was over. I darted for the cafeteria and tried not to make eye contact with the men in black.

Ten years later, I returned to that same campground—no longer a longhair, but not dressed in black, either. One of those men from that auctioneer altar kidded me as I made my way to the platform to give the main address for the evening—"Well looky here," as he squeezed my cheek, "Who would have thought this. I think the Red Sea has parted again."

Through it all, these men in black introduced me to the "why" behind their austere actions—a deep desire to give every aspect of their lives to Christ. They told me that when people become saved (which later I learned meant to become Christians), the Holy Spirit comes into their lives. As they grow in Christ, they come to a point in which they realize more fully what that new relationship means. At that point, they choose to become "entirely sanctified."

When they told me this, I was still trying to figure out who Christ is/was, and the very word "sanctified" sounded cultish. Scared me. In Buck Creek, "Jesus Christ!" was a common expletive, and multisyllabic words like "sanctified" (and multisyllabic) had no currency.

Regardless of the cultural shifts, the biblical message and challenge to be set apart for Christ speaks to each generation. It takes on different forms, and every generation will have those who appear legalistic and those who appear too socially liberal. Both groups read the same Bible and follow the same Lord. And this dynamic plays out among the different stripes of Judaism as well, with its liberals and conservatives, and ultra-conservative branches (and colleges).

Many of those black-cloaked preachers from that memorable tabernacle moment are now in heaven. Several of them, and those still living, have become friends.

I realize that those altars that looked like they stretched from here to eternity—probably do. The men in black and I look different as we kneel and in the frequency of our kneeling but not in why we do so.

Regardless of your religious beliefs, the next time you kneel I hope you reflect not so much on what you're doing or how good you are at it, but why.

Buck Creek Wisdom #10

"If the Why is big enough, the How will show up."

"We look on the outward appearance but God looks at the heart, but oftentimes we claim to see peoples' hearts on their sleeves."

"Regardless of the cultural shifts and time separating us from religious traditions, the biblical challenge to be set apart for Christ speaks to each generation."

"In an era championing tolerance, it's counterintuitive to dismiss unfamiliar biblical talk as ephemeral gibberish while many nations have considered it a language of eternal significance."

Buck Creek & the Bible

Two major differences between Western societies (like in the U.S.) and that of the Old and New Testament authors are the role of elders and the prevalence of young leaders. Each year, the media highlights the newest billionaires under 30 years old or the most promising teen millionaires. This rise of young success stories doesn't change the role of wise elders. The Bible's setting throughout its centuries of writing remained patriarchal, with much emphasis on the senior male in the family line. These texts are replete with instructions to obey both our parents and elders in general. "Stand up in the presence of the aged, show respect for the elderly and revere your God. I am the Lord." (Leviticus 19: 32) While economic structures and opportunities have changed drastically since the time of Moses, King David, St. Paul and the other writers, human nature hasn't.

CHAPTER ELEVEN:
An Afro at the Crossroads

Our 1966 Buck Creek classroom was predictable.
Kathy sitting by the radiator biting her flat eraser. Bruce drawing the rocklike form of *Fantastic Four's* The Thing. Ned staring at the graveyard through the four-foot second story window. Big Jim whispering to Big Ben. My cousin John passing notes. Tim sneaking a taste of *Elmer's* glue

You could always find the silver pencil sharpener mounted between the slate blackboard and dark door trim and the round, generic clock centered above the teacher's substantial oak desk.

Glancing across the rows of flip-top desks, you would see a bubbly assortment of classmates. Red hair. Blonde hair. Freckles. Quasi-rich. Mostly poor. All white.

We never thought twice about the latter. That's the way it was. It was all we knew. "Diversity" may have been a word—somewhere—but it was neither a cause nor a curricular concern.

Not much changed in our neck of the woods throughout the 1960s and 70s. While Selma was sizzling with racial protests, many northern towns were conspicuously silent. Discussion of segregation and equality was for Atlanta and Little Rock and for their teachers, politicians and police—not for the Buck Creeks scattered throughout the rural north, at least not among elementary kids.

It would be years before we became aware of such matters.

The first non-White in any class wouldn't come until late in high school. Blacks were found in *National Geographic* and big cities. Paths between Buck Creek and Motown rarely crossed.

"The only colored folks we ever saw," reflected an eighty-year-old Buck Creek alumnus, "were the rail workers whose sleeper car pulled off the tracks here. We played 'em in softball. Watched 'em closely, and they behaved themselves—perfect gentlemen. Those were memorable games."

You can imagine the buzz around Buck Creek when my sister "went and found her one of them colored men"— recounted my uncle while hunting sponge mushrooms.

I smile today at the irony of raising my family for many years in the historic black community of Weaver, originally called Crossroads—six miles south of Marion, Indiana.

Faded pictures reveal a general store, three churches, a school, a landing strip for a lone crop duster, a horse track and many social functions. About all that remains today is a cemetery where over two thousand are buried on a half-acre plot (county road 600 South).

By 1920, most of the families from this community had moved a few miles north to Marion—new laws permitted them equal access to public schools.

The saddest irony occurred in 1930. Within months of officially closing its town status, former residents of Crossroads witnessed a lynching in their newly desegregated home of Marion.

Equality in education was not synonymous with civility.

America knows of the lynching and the alleged past KKK presence twenty miles south of Marion. It also knows of James Dean's home a few miles east. Weaver is poised as a crossroads in history and between divergent values and causes.

My four boys passed daily through the Weaver (Crossroads) intersection. On every passing, their lives intersected with the history of racism and the cause of equality—a dynamic I've termed in my books the "Crossroads Principle."

When our lives personally intersect an issue or an aspect of a cause, experiential learning takes place. We have a chance to personalize the learning—what educators say is the key to a deeper understanding.

My eldest son chose Rosa Parks as the subject of a major paper. He found that the same values she held while sitting on that Alabama bus were connected to our town.

These values once plowed the soil of our own farm and the rest of Crossroads' plots. He knows that Crossroads was more than a name for a black community. It was a need for a people's survival. It was a divergence in values.

The Crossroads Principle occurs not only for those who drove past our farm, but also whenever teachers reflect on a class roster or the selection of curriculum.

It happens when your black son brings home a white girlfriend, or when you plan a block party Saturday night, forgetting your neighbor's Sabbath.

It occurred when America heard a sportscaster talk about the breeding of a race for sports and an Indiana University coach apologized for inadvertent comments offending whites. It's also when a local landlord denies rent to a new family because of race and when you build a Habitat for Humanity home for a former classmate.

We fly through crossroads weekly, if not daily. We're occasionally blindsided. The hope is that we become more aware of the intersections, and that through these passages we better navigate the journey.

My relatives now hold reunions where the Buck Creek School stood. Recently, several families pulled away from the crushed-stone parking lot and began their homeward treks through the worn crossroad at town center.

I noticed a Buck Creek boy pausing on his bicycle long enough to watch this rare flurry of traffic.

The boy's head turned to my sister's car ahead of us. My niece's wind-blown Afro filled nearly half the rear window as she turned to wave goodbye.

Was the young onlooker's perspective one of curiosity of the unfamiliar, like mine forty years earlier? Was he more preoccupied with the number of cars passing than the color of the passengers? Was this serendipitous intersection with another race his only diversity crossroads, with no intentional ones at school, church or home?

We try to prepare for intersections. At times, we plan them.

Perhaps we need to hand the wheel to a friend while we press our faces against the rear glass and reflect on what crossed our path.

Intentionally or unintentionally, intersections should help our introspection.

Buck Creek Wisdom #11

"The Crossroads Principle: In order to embrace an ideal you need to be able to get your mind around it."

"Looking out the back window usually helps to understand better what's on the road ahead."

"Facilitating internal motivation is a matter of identifying crossroads, when the values of noble causes intersect with personal experiences."

"When a value becomes a priority that drives concerted actions around it—the cause—then that value becomes an ideal for that cause."

Buck Creek & the Bible

"The Last Supper" has become one of the most famous meals in history from its historical and biblical setting to its image in Leonardo Di Vinci's painting. During this event in Jerusalem around AD 30, Jesus had reminded his Disciples that he was about to leave earth—something that is understandably hard for a group to comprehend without knowing the end of the story (his crucifixion and resurrection or the "Good Friday" and "Easter" stories). At that same table he also dealt directly with Judas Iscariot, associated in history with the likes of Benedict Arnold—the worst of traitors. In the recorded text (which has extant evidence early in the second century), just a few sentences later and after Judas "was gone," Jesus said, "A new command I give you: Love one another. As I have loved you, so you must love one another. By this everyone will know that you are my disciples, if you love one another." (John 13: 34-35) Whether Christians are with people from different cultures, ethnicities and/or socio-economic backgrounds, the command and ideal is to love them.

CHAPTER TWELVE:
Throwing Away Prize Possessions

I threw my sister's best friend down the outhouse hole.

Running through the torn screen door, I reached the john ahead of my screaming sibling and hastily laid-to-rest her favorite soft plastic toy in a smelly grave.

With a delayed thud in the dark underworld, victory was mine. Gone was the bright blue Easter bunny that had once illuminated our two-story, crumbling-brick home.

Then, this towheaded boy in the outhouse turned. Mom's familiar silhouette blocked the door, and my triumph ended.

Her willow-branch discipline began.

One set of cheeks tear stained, the other set numb—and the real drama hadn't begun. My strong-forearmed mother-of-eight conscripted a volunteer for a memorable rescue—my lanky, long-legged cousin Lurch.

He almost snagged the lifeless squeaker toy by lowering the lye can on a worn cotton clothesline rope. Lurch persisted while biting the end of a mammoth metal flashlight. Eventually, I held both the light and my nose until Mom dismissed me.

His "Plan B" called for the removal of the worn wooden seat. In Ray Romano fashion, sensibility gave way to challenge. Lurch was braving the murky depths to rescue a little girl's best friend. Hero status seemed within his grasp.

There were plenty of stories about our friends falling into outhouse pits in Buck Creek, Indiana, especially after Halloween pranksters scooted back the johns.

And poor cousin Jeffery lived with a septic stigmatization. He failed his double-dare jump over an open, overfull pit with the entire lid removed. Laughter subsided as he began to sink—his shoulders disappeared, and his head was soon to follow.

Parents ran. Rescue ensued. Willow branches flew. Bottoms were blue.

Lurch, now perspiring, proceeded nonetheless. He leaned all the more precariously into the abyss—every attempt more daring.

Then he coughed, slipped, and bolted for our outdoor water pump.

He worked the pump lever furiously and thought the ordeal was over.

Then Lurch had that look men get when they're about to make history for the wrong reasons.

Arising, staring at the door with the intensity of my Uncle Buck's hounds at treed raccoons, we all knew that this effort was closer to the beginning than the end.

Lurch dismantled a bit more of the interior—figuring that he could hold onto the john floor, place his feet on adjoining sides of the pit, and then pluck the now pitiful rabbit from the mire.

A ragtag crowd gathered—moms with hip-hugging infants, *Salem*-smoking grandmas, Buck Creek bullies, Little Rascal look-alikes, an aunt in a daisy apron.

All seemed to be going well until his Dingo Boot slipped on the slick wall.

Like trying to climb a metal silo in mid-August with slabs of bacon on his feet, Lurch was in trouble. His filterless Camels fell from his soiled t-shirt sleeve. His countenance changed from John Wayne conquering the evil john to an uncensored Jacky Gleason.

It wasn't Jesus' name he was yelling, it was Jerry's.

Cousin or not, flailing away in yucky boots beneath an outhouse while staring at his soggy smokes and a now sarcastic, smiling, pudgy rabbit—the biggest, "baddest" kid in town was steaming.

Lurch failed. My sister wailed. The backyard stank. The stupid rabbit sank.

The irony is that I loved that silly rabbit.

Through a childish rage, I discarded our prized possession. It was a bright spot amidst our drab nine-dollar-a-month rental home.

In our only family picture from my elementary years—taken on the sofa in that one-time storefront building—I'm holding the soft, blue and white, sad-eyed bunny.

I can still see the bright rabbit's contrast against its murky grave, encircled by the flashlight beam.

It's a contrast played out in many forms throughout history.

The pure and virgin alongside the defiled and prostituted, the noble flanked by the ignoble. Too often we hear of prize possessions selfishly and senselessly discarded and bright hallmarks of the humane buried beneath the inhumane.

I was all of five years old, and since have learned to value uplifting things and to uplift values. To recognize the contrast between the bright and the banal. To distinguish between the serene and the sordid. I can laugh about the childhood incident, a basic life lesson.

However, failure to learn lessons of contrasts and consequences is a step toward incivility, and like standing over a sinking cousin, fear should supplant laughter.

The world's Saddams balked at these lessons, laughing at evil and at dissenting voices.

No longer children, they still discarded valuable possessions. Not childish things, but human beings. Not toys, but girls and boys. And with morally platonic smiles they listened for delayed thuds in the mire.

The late Saddam no longer flinched at the sulfurous smell from the dark side of contrasts. He promoted his own face while effacing his own bloodline.

He controlled much of the world's gas, but gassed his own people. He called for harmony among Arabs, but attacked Arab nations.

Instead of fueling educational reform, he burned his uneducated, frightened people with kerosene.

And Basran families, afraid of the fight, were gunned down in flight.

He violated Iraqi women, raped Iraq and mistook palaces for prized possessions.

The Hanging Gardens of Babylon were nearly forgotten in the shadow of hanging captives in Baghdad. Beautiful mosques were flanked by morgues of the mutilated where tongues had been nailed to posts near barren fields.

Saddam ignored contrasts and millions paid the consequences. As we struggle with the aftermath of unseating a Saddam and in the light of human rights' violators like Iran's Mahmoud Ahmadinejad, let's not forget the mounds of tortured corpses and the noble U.S. military's fight for what is right. It's not only a Western value nor only an American goal; their fight for human dignity and the survival of the helpless is basic humanitarianism.

To close the blinds to the slaughter, rape or human trafficking of children, whether in Iraq, Afghanistan, Cambodia or Rwanda, is to slam the window to hope. Shall the best of American education help our future politicians to recognize and create humanitarian windows through which the disenfranchised can escape—including in our own house?

We have all run through life's childish screen doors and have thrown precious possessions beneath outhouse floors. But the Saddams of the world make so many trips to outhouse holes, they eventually deposit their long-faded souls. Losing one's soul leads to a vacuous social and moral conscience.

Buck Creek Wisdom #12

"It's easy to be stigmatized when you play around sewer."

"Failure to learn lessons about contrasts and consequences is a step toward incivility."

"No matter our level of education or public position, the law of non-contradiction still applies: two opposing views cannot both be true at the same time and in the same respect."

"It's counterintuitive to think we can always have consensus, especially when some people are wrong by belief and others through deceit."

Buck Creek & the Bible

As I'm entering my mid-50s, the silliness of possessions is becoming all the more apparent. As more of my relatives and friends pass away, I'm reminded of the foolishness of material things. And, as an ancient historian who has been to numerous archaeological sites, I'm rather familiar with what happens with nice homes, furniture, and personal items with the passage of time (some whole civilizations have been lost, and even the pharaohs couldn't entomb their wealth indefinitely). Jesus instructs us, "Do not store up for yourselves treasures on earth, where moths and vermin destroy, and where thieves break in and steal. But store up for yourselves treasures in heaven, where moths and vermin do not destroy, and where thieves do not break in and steal. For where your treasure is, there your heart will be also." (Matthew 6: 19-21)

Dr. Jerry Pattengale

CHAPTER THIRTEEN:
Falling on a Deer Ruins the Surprise

When my uncle landed on the deer, the surprise was over!

He fell from his tree stand, a hunting blind, and the poor deer didn't know what hit him. It ran off while my uncle remained with several broken ribs and a bruised pride.

Imagine that deer's conversation when he rejoined his herd. "Some camouflaged flying man covered in deer urine came from nowhere—didn't see it coming." And an older deer likely responded, "Yeah, strange things seem to happen in those woods near Buck Creek. I once saw a dude in the bushes with a rifle and a hat with antlers—he needs to start watching Bill Dance."

For the next three decades, my uncle's buddies hurled jokes. "Hey, grab your saddle and let's go hunting." Or, "Are we taking my truck or did you rent an ambulance?" "I see your rifle, got your parachute?"

That routine hunting trip became legendary. He was drawing back his bow when, according to him, the largest buck he had seen in years stopped directly beneath him. As he maneuvered for the most unpredictable shot, one you never plan for, he was suddenly airborne.

57

It was tough for people to be serious while visiting my recovering uncle. "Hey, is the deer okay?" People snickered in the kitchen as they discussed his situation over Euchre games, and occasionally yelled to him over their dangling cigarettes and squinting eyes, "Did the game warden fine you for jumping deer out of season?" "Did you ever think of landing feet first?" "It was bad enough ya fell on the thing, but then you had to tell us! The boys at the VFW will sure be glad to see ya." And my favorite, "Why didn't you drop an anvil on him, like in the *Roadrunner*?"

One uncle quit razzing him when word got out that he got punched by his wife but this time because of a falling deer! My aunt and uncle were madly in love, and their only fight happened while he was sleeping. Yep, when his prized deer head fell from the wall above their bed and onto her head, my small feisty aunt slugged her beloved with all her might. "Trophy" wife jokes ensued.

Whether falling from a blind onto a deer or being blindsided by a falling buck, unexpected and spontaneous moments can hit hard.

Sometimes the smallest decisions during a routine day change lives. Some off-the-cuff comment. A split decision. An email. Isaiah Thomas' "B____" comment, Dan Quayle's "potatoe," Rodney King's "Can't we all just get along?" and a host of others are comments that changed lives. The same with Kelly Pickler's "calamari" comment on *American Idol*. Doug Flute's last pass for Boston College. Woody Haye's punching of IU's no. 58 on the Ohio State sideline. Kanye West's imbecilic Taylor Swift comment.

I suppose those moments are a lot like hunting—unexpected even when you plan. The suddenness. The rush. And usually your reaction, whether you hit or miss the deer, is part of the challenge.

And we all have stories about spontaneous incidents or accidents. For all of us there's that day when the unexpected happens. We're likely not falling on deer but on our faces. An email sent to the wrong person, or to the wrong list. A slipped thought or response. A private vote made public. A virtual incident with public manifestation. A confidence accidentally betrayed, or an accident kept in confidence.

The measure of a man or woman is what's done in private. What's done in private often manifests itself unexpectedly in public.

Tim Elmore's *Habitudes* are built around living more consistent (and virtuous) lives (www.timelmore.com). And, ones in which spontaneous actions match deep convictions. One of his Habitudes, the "Waldorf Principle," captures this well. It's named after the story of George C. Boldt who was running a small boutique inn when an older couple stopped in during a rainstorm; they had been unable to find a room due to a major conference in nearby Philadelphia. George's modest hotel was full, and regretted he had no room in the inn. As the couple began to walk back into the storm, George stopped them and convinced them to take his room for the night. It was still clean, and he insisted until they accepted.

The next morning the couple, the Waldorfs, informed George that they had never been treated with such sacrificial kindness. "I might just build one of the finest hotels in the world, and if I do, I want you to run it." And, years later, George received a plane ticket to New York to run the elegant Waldorf-Astoria Hotel. Boldt's decisions have likely intersected with your life through the Waldorf Salad or Thousand Island dressing appearing first on his menu.

A spontaneous decision rooted in genuine concern for people had lasting consequences. Ordinary days like that of George Boldt can have extraordinary significance.

On an otherwise routine day a deer broke my uncle's fall, perhaps saved his life, but couldn't help him save face. Thirty-five years later the Buck Creek elders still shake their heads about deer jumping. Spontaneous moments go both ways, but whether negative or positive, falling on deer, slipping with phrases, or sacrificing a room, they really are rarely accidents. And as for my aunt, she was just happy her husband didn't hunt moose.

Buck Creek Wisdom #13

"Sometimes the smallest decision during a routine day changes lives in a major way."

"Where and how hard you fall is usually determined by where you stand."

"The deeper you go spiritually, the more consistent you are spontaneously."

"Many consequential policies stem from inconsequential practices."

Buck Creek & the Bible

We've likely all done some silly things in private, though I can only think of one person who has fallen on a deer. Likewise, we also have done our share of good deeds. The "Sermon on the Mount" begins with these words from Jesus, "Be careful not to practice your righteousness in front of others to be seen by them. If you do, you will have no reward from your Father in heaven. So when you give to the needy, do not announce it with trumpets, as the hypocrites do in the synagogues and on the streets, to be honored by others. Truly I tell you, they have received their reward in full. But when you give to the needy, do not let your left hand know what your right hand is doing, so that your giving may be in secret. Then your Father, who sees what is done in secret, will reward you." (Matthew 6: 2-4)

Dr. Jerry Pattengale

CHAPTER FOURTEEN:
Buck Creek English and Life Rhythms

"Thud!" The large lady's attempt at robbery failed when the ham fell from beneath her dress and hit the floor. Instead of walking away, my friend said that the ham burglar stood alone in the aisle and began yelling "Who be hittin' me with a ham?! Don't be a-throwin' hams at me! Betta don't! Betta don't be throwin' hams at me. I'm tellin' ya now, betta don't! . . . Betta don't!"

This isn't right on so many levels, and yelling "Betta don't!" signals wanton wisdom and learning on many fronts. It's no wonder that a collegian-favorite website is "People of Wal-Mart."

While I can't relate to stuffing a ham up my clothes, I was reminded of my own grammatical journey from the Buck Creek woods to wooden college desks. The university "didn't have no" category for my language. "They" really "should of" recognized my giftedness, "to really encourage" how I had "been schooled."

A *dangling participle* sounded like someone who needed rescued, and *syntax* like something you'd talk about with your priest and IRS agent. *Allegory* seemed fitting for a Halloween movie, and phrases like "punitive damages" made us giggle.

"What did you come here to college for?" sounded like a perfectly good question, instead of my professor's version—"Why did you choose to attend this college?" The truth was, I understood both sentences and so did he.

I assume that many routines in Ms. Betta Don't's life influenced that moment, and the same was true of Buck Creek routines. School 'til at least junior high school, fishing and hunting instead of SAT preparation, stock car races, chopping wood, hunting night crawlers, and if you "had a bun in the oven" it was "yours to take care of." No Planned Parenthood, but rather planning with parents while sitting on car hoods. No "Right to Life" fights, just matter-of-fact right things to do for new lives and young wives.

Thirty years later, many of my teen peers are still in similar jobs, etching out an honest but modest living. At reunions I often hear, "Yeah, Jerry Allen, I should have *went* to college, but . . ." Or, "I *seen* what was gonna happen back then, but . . ." Like me, most are children of teens. Most are beautiful people, though there remain some who are real rascals and some in jail. About half still have at least half their teeth. About half own homes and remain married to their teen brides. And, some are doing rather well in about every way possible—including mastering English as a second language.

Routines shape us. We can hear it on others' lips. See it in their teeth. Smell it on their clothes. Observe it in their kids.

Dorothy Bass describes this dynamic of routines in her book, *Receiving the Day*. I had the privilege recently of thanking her over breakfast for helping me to understand anew what she calls "life rhythms." She writes about the Hebrew children's forty-year journey in the desert and the role of gathering manna six days a week. According to Exodus, on the sixth day of the week they would gather twice as much manna ("out of nothing"), so that they had enough to eat on the Sabbath—helping to establish the rhythm of the Sabbath still with us.

She also writes of a father who realized that the routine question, "How did your day go?" seemed to miss the mark, and began asking "Where did God meet you today?"

While Buck Creek had its grammar oddities and was wanton in some basic cosmopolitan practices, some wonderful rhythms remain precious memories. Sitting for hours on a riverbank while grandpa talked about nature often beginning with "Jerry Allen, did I ever tell you about . . ." Sharing family evenings around a long dinner table. Weekends listening to my uncles' ingenious banjo songs. All long pauses from their otherwise long, rugged lives.

Recently, L. Gregory Jones (Dean of Duke Divinity School) shared a true story on our campus about an experiment with monkeys. At first they'd all scamper up the pole and devour the bananas at the top. However, the scientists then rigged the bananas to douse the monkeys with water. Eventually, they quit climbing. Then, they rotated one of the four monkeys out and brought in a new one. As the novice monkey got excited about the fruit and began to climb, the other three pulled him down. In time, all four of the original monkeys had been rotated out, and yet they kept all new monkeys from climbing the pole.

At times, we all need to look anew at our routines. And, like Dorothy suggests, begin to establish some healthy life rhythms.

My cousin Danny (Dee) and his wife Henrietta (Henry) grace the beautiful, non-descript backwater Buck Creek community. They're in their mid fifties and are still madly in love after nearly forty years. A few years ago, they helped a PBS film crew with a movie about my Buck Creek upbringing, and I'd often see hands interlocked, constant smiles, deep eye contact, kissing, and hugging with newlywed passion. They're good people, beautiful people, inside and out. And, they're very happy. (This book is dedicated to Danny.)

They've established some wonderful life rhythms. Besides sound morals and personal character, they fill a room with joy—whether it's decorated in fine China or scratched Tupperware. During the filming (*Leading the Way out of Poverty*), I asked Danny about his kids. This handsome, rugged man with a soft smile stood near his plastic deer target and piles of chopped wood and shared an amazing life rhythm.

It was no surprise that his wife and kids were at his life's center. He's worked the same job of maintaining county roads that he landed during his teen years. But he also has raised four kids and awarded each with a house and a car when they finished high school. His life rhythm was in tune with his kids' futures, and he had learned from the education void in his own journey.

I've had the privilege of working directly with some of the world's wealthiest families, and here stood before me a man who perhaps hadn't been able to climb the pole, but made sure in a more pronounced way that he wasn't the one pulling back his children.

En route back from Chicago, my colleagues and I headed east from I-65 and Route 18 in Indiana, and eventually cut through Buck Creek to intersect Route 26. There was Danny in army fatigues, hunting cap, and thick leather gloves running a wood splitter—alongside his son-in-law. He paused and yelled, "Well looky there, it's Jerry Allen! What brings ya to this neck of the woods with a bunch of Hillbillies?" It never crossed my mind to correct his grammar. Rather, I jumped out and hugged a real man that day. One whose life rhythms knew the value of work and play, of perspective and pausing for first-rate priorities.

And if you see me in Wal-Mart this week, it's not a ham stuffed up my shirt—that's tangible evidence of a deep-fried Buck Creek dietary rhythm.

Buck Creek Wisdom #14

"If a picture is worth a thousand words, then write with illustrations."

"High culture is determined by the quality of a table's talk not its linens."

"Our life rhythms correlate with our lasting countenance."

Buck Creek & the Bible

One of the most-accessed verses on the internet (through www.BibleGateway.com) relates to the routines of life: "Finally, brothers, whatever is true, whatever is noble, whatever is right, whatever is pure, whatever is lovely, whatever is admirable—if anything is excellent or praiseworthy—think about such things." (Philippians 4:8)

CHAPTER FIFTEEN:
The Buck Creek Diet

In Buck Creek, we ate the darndest things. Instead of wasting weed killer on dandelions, my uncle fed them to us under the pretense of herbal delights. The only "herb" I was certain about lived down the lane with teeth as scarce as Gary Hart posters. Herb's diet left him with less enamel than Indiana Jones' nuked refrigerator.

Boiled snapper ranked among the ugliest dishes, sort of a mushy cauliflower, and you needed a dipstick to check the oil in muskrat filets. Elephant ear mushrooms resembled tree fungus on steroids. We called our venison skewers "Bambi on a stick."

Fried potato sandwiches, corn pancakes, wild onion stew, and pig rinds (cracklings) were our staples, along with breaded tenderloins pulverized more than President Obama's Cairo Speech.

Buffet tables at weekend gatherings sported pigs' feet fit for *Blair Witch Project* props, corn popped in bacon grease, Bannie hen egg omelets, whole milk straight from the whole cow, rib-sticking biscuits and gravy, velvet cakes, and if we were lucky, *Kool-Aid* sprinkled over homemade ice cream—on sugar-laced rhubarb pie.

Yeah, ya might as well have stuck a lard-filled syringe straight into our aortas. Speaking of lard, we saved it in old *Folgers'* cans and stretched it longer than George Will's sentences. Those were the days, when broiling chicken was about as sacrilegious as criticizing someone for deep-frying catfish from the Wabash River.

Somehow my grandfather lived ninety-nine years, but many others had long since passed from heart failures, including my dad in his early fifties. What may have tasted great as a child can leave a bad taste decades later. We knew as much about trans fats and cholesterol as we did about SAT preparation and college rankings.

At my fiftieth birthday party, I opened the fridge and saw a dietary abomination—a carton of *Soymilk*. I didn't know whether to puke or salute. In Buck Creek, we would have joked about "how to milk a soybean."

But my five decades have helped me to learn that tasteful things can do bad things to the taster. For many years, I was faithful to exercising, even appeared with my weightlifting friend Randy Holt on the "Jerry's Kids" TV telethons, but all the while my Buck Creek diet was still with me, destroying me from within.

The "good old days" are often irresponsible memories. Reflection isn't always 20/20, and countless families continue with cultural blinders. My relatives fed us a balanced diet—it's just that the scales were greased and "balance" redefined.

I hope to live as long as grandpa who worked into his nineties. He retired from his first job forty years after liberating German concentration camps and being maimed by a landmine. Ironically, he spent his career repairing his own county's roads. His second career (two more decades) was sacking groceries at the Delphi IGA. In addition to the Buck Creek diet, he chewed cheap cigars for half a century. No rhyme or reason, the diet seems to have slid through his veins much easier than for many of us.

I'm overdue for my fifty-year check up, and I'm sure my doctor will order me actually to start drinking that sad soy stuff instead of pouring it on our flowers. I've already gone to skim milk in coffee, and he'll probably tell me something silly like "caffeine is bad for you." I've only had one cigarette and one beer my entire life, but boy have I overdosed on those plaque builders.

I'm writing this on the eve of Thanksgiving, and more than taste is being stripped from our cultural diet—just as *Christ*mas sentiments are being emasculated in many communities, our Thanksgiving holiday is being rewritten without any supernatural connection. I'm not talking about the move to socializing healthcare, but about socializing spirituality—neutering our human condition, as if it were possible.

Taking socialized spirituality to its logical conclusion, we'll be gathering 'round the dinner table, all equally, and all with the same amount of financial and personal input. I suppose in the Buck Creeks of America we'll take the lard and high-caloric discards and shape a Socialism Idol. Yeah, instead of facing a cruciform nave while praying, rolling out mats and bowing east or lighting a seven-branched candle, we'll be placing that collective sterile god between us and the liberal Chicago-area winds and pay homage to our bland and bleak future. The "courage to hope" without supernatural help is like idolizing the best and worst of us—whether it's a hardened lard idol or a glitzy Wall Street icon, both ephemeral at best, and lethal at worst.

No lard idol this Thanksgiving at the Buck Creek table. Nope, instead I'll have special placemats on our long dining table with the full "Thanksgiving Mandate" from George Washington, the first federal mandate given to this great nation (City of New York, October 3, 1789), which begins with, "Whereas it is the duty of all Nations to acknowledge the providence of Almighty God, to obey his will, to be grateful for his benefits, and humbly to implore his protection and favor, and . . . by acknowledging with grateful hearts the many signal favors of Almighty God . . . ."

It's not my own wellbeing that concerns me most, but that of our children and one day being there for our grandchildren. And this includes a diet for their spiritual wellbeing as well, as Washington wrote, "to promote the knowledge and practice of true religion and virtue."

In the meantime, I think I'll ask the good doctor to file off my taste buds and pass me all that's bland.

Buck Creek Wisdom #15

"If you are what you eat then you're full of yourself."

"A simple diet helps protect against expensive tastes."

"Romanticizing the past is often irresponsible recall, as hindsight isn't always 20/20."

"Socializing spirituality neuters our human condition."

Buck Creek & the Bible

Although I joke about eating deep-fried food, which is still an occasional treat, the seriousness of health has settled in for both practical and spiritual reasons. "Do you not know that your body is a temple of the Holy Spirit, who is in you, whom you have received from God? You are not your own." (1 Corinthians 6:19) This passage is often used to discuss drugs, illicit sex, and many other decisions that might have negative effects on one's body (and mind). And, it's often a trite sarcastic reprimand for someone eating french-fries.

Dr. Jerry Pattengale

CHAPTER SIXTEEN:
Buck Creek Track

Only one time in my lackluster track career did I pass our school's best runner—and in fact everyone did, head on.

Our track star was a pothead with a magnetic smile. He disguised his addiction until that infamous day on the track. When the gun sounded for the 1500, he somehow managed to run gracefully, but in the wrong direction.

The event was surrealistic. The race occurred while scraggly students in seventies clothes whistled and yelled. We had lined up with our star teammate, and the surfer-looking jokester had us all laughing. He had a smooth style, and the race had always come easy.

It was a windy day, and his flowing mullet made him appear even more relaxed. At that moment, we all knew that he was untouchable. He had dominated every race, every meet. He was long legged and over six foot. I was an anemic 5'8". His legs had muscles that separated with every step. My legs looked like two strings hanging from my belt. He had the GQ face with a strong jaw. I had more of a DQ look and the body of a straw.

He was still chatting when the gun sounded, standing there with arms folded. His confidence was unnerving. I rounded the first turn and caught a glimpse of his pronounced style—but on the other end of the track. A couple of runners were smiling. We all thought he was joking. As he neared us he was unusually happy, but noticeably disoriented.

Concern supplanted humor.

He circled the cinder track before the teachers could stop him. I can't remember who won that race because the loser was so pronounced. A gifted runner would not return to the track—ever.

The race continued: our feet were moving but our heads were spinning. The image of adults scampering to protect our friend from himself was alarming. It's a sad bookmark from my Buck Creek days. I wish there were a happy ending to the story, but that was the end of the story—he was expelled from junior high and never returned to our system and struggled for years.

In track, he broke a rule that disqualified him to run. In school, he had broken a rule that barred him from participation.

I'm now in my mid-fifties and have since witnessed another promising individual running the wrong direction—an Episcopal priest. He, too, was unnerving, but for a strikingly different reason—he didn't look disoriented. He looked confident. In fact, he was happy and gay, and shouted about a new outpouring of God's love along the way. Before the gun sounded, a group of people told him it was okay to run contrary to the established religious rules.

At some point in his training, it seems that someone would have explained to him the rules. Someone early in the process certainly thought about calling him aside and sharing that although he has the right to practice a gay lifestyle, he's in a race that has rules fundamental to the event's very survival.

At some point, his coaches and mentors were taken by his charisma and failed to separate personality from principle, and slighted the latter. Long before he stepped into the public arena, the rules were challenged. In time, they were changed.

Anyone can go to a track and run counterclockwise, but if you want to be a part of the universal sport of track and field, you'll be disqualified. A group, whether two or two million, might like your direction better. Maybe they're tired of watching people always running right and leaning left.

Just as new sports and new sports leagues are organized, from *Fantasy* and *X-games* to *Slamball*, the Episcopal Church of America (ECA) has that prerogative to start an organization separate from orthodox Christianity. And the same is true more recently for the Evangelical Lutheran Church of America (ELCA). In 2009, this 4.6 million-member denomination voted to accept gay and lesbian pastors in "committed relationships" (curiously redefining the biblical injunction against homosexuality). The question is not whether those involved in the decision to commission a gay priest are well meaning, or whether the priest is educationally qualified. Rather, it's whether they have violated moral rules basic to established (orthodox) Christianity.

In *Straight Talk,* I champion the common definition of "orthodox" (from Greek *orth*: straight, true; and *doxa*: opinion): "religious teachings and practices that conform to the established doctrine of the Church, i.e., that do not contradict the essence of the Apostles' Creed, the Biblical canon, and the officially approved doctrines unique to the relative main movement of Christianity."

The ECA and ECLA are headed in a different direction than that of orthodox teaching, hitting it head on. Instead of zealous youths in mullets cheering from the stands, there are highly educated elders taking unorthodox stands. It's one thing to proclaim "love" and to endorse "tolerance," but another to take them to "an unwarranted extreme"—the essence of a heresy. When the cause of love changes rules established by the divine dispenser of love (well, according to an orthodox view), then a misguided venture occurs.

The same Bible that underpins orthodoxy calls Christians to "run the good race." Some denominations are running, but in a different race than the Apostle Paul endorses. In this age of relativism, perhaps they'll say, we "have run the good *compromised* race," while pastors sing the old spiritual, "We've got good reason to be happy and gay"— because they can.

Buck Creek Wisdom #16

"Make decisions on principle and not personality."

"If you pass the leader head on, someone is running the wrong race."

"One's open mindedness does not determine biblical orthodoxy."

Buck Creek & the Bible

The Bible is rather clear about the power and clarity of its message, and that we are held accountable by its laws, not whether we agree with them. "For the word of God is living and active. Sharper than any double-edged sword, it penetrates even to dividing soul and spirit, joints and marrow; it judges the thoughts and attitudes of the heart." (Hebrews 4:12) Believing in biblical commands is not a negative proposition, but one replete with promises, not least of which is eternal life. "For God so loved the world that he gave his one and only Son, that whoever believes in him shall not perish but have eternal life. For God did not send his Son into the world to condemn the world, but to save the world through him." (John 3:16-17)

CHAPTER SEVENTEEN:
Christmas in Buck Creek, Indiana

Sitting in the back of Purdue's Memorial Union, a "happy thought" of Peter Pan lore struck me. "I have been here before," I recalled, "nearly forty years ago, during my Buck Creek days." Listen in, forty years back.

When the bell for Christmas break sounded, we ran from our festive Buck Creek School to our snub-nose bus wearing our hand-me-down, penniless loafers and earmuffs.

Nearly a decade passed before I realized that the holidays weren't so happy for Buck Creek adults. Many of our parents were laid off; it was our teachers who had ensured a stable place during the season. Many presents "From Mom and Dad" were actually "From the Teacher," though they never let on.

One year the school Christmas tree cut from the adjacent woods reached to the high cracked-plastered ceiling. The angel cap fit only at an angle. It was the first time I had seen a color wheel—the latest in technology. That flimsy piece of cardboard with colored plastic inserts brought the tinseled tree to life. It mesmerized us second graders.

At the school's gift exchange, we all hoped that Judy would draw our name. She came from the biggest house and usually gave the nicest gifts. I wrapped the standard package of green WWII soldiers—quantity somehow seemed to look like quality. Also, skinny Santa came to the Buck Creek School annually—after we heard that Jesus was the "reason for the season." Besides Easter, that was my annual dose of religion.

We never seemed to notice that Santa had the same snaggletooth smile as our school janitor.

One memorable Christmas, our quasi-fatherless family hunkered down again for the long school break. After the stability of the semester ended, eight kids crowded into our house. Dad had our only car and the only license—he thought a woman's place was in the home. Until the divorce, that's exactly where Mom stayed. He refueled at the tavern more often than the Americus Shell station. At twenty-eight cents per gallon, gas was certainly a better deal than mugs of Falls City across the street.

That particular cold, biting winter, Dad and most other carpenters had little work. He seemed to imbibe more than usual while we got on with Christmas break. At home, board games, taffy pulls, and no-bake cookies somehow disguised our Spartan festivities.

The carpenters' union invited us to its Christmas party—at Purdue's expansive Memorial Union—the very room where I found myself decades later. Mom borrowed clothes for us kids, and my grandpa surprised me with a "G.I." (butch) haircut.

The night on Purdue's campus was like a dream. Long tables decked in fine cutlery and loaded with food. A scraggly assortment of kids. A giant tree surrounded by colorful boxes. And, a big jolly Santa with all his teeth. Some of the carpenters' wives seemed to know all of our names. We were referred to as "The Pattengale kids," one of the "special families." I now understand that eight young kids and no work qualified us as "*special.*"

I stared at the presents and gazed at the expansive North Ballroom. I didn't know such buildings existed in Indiana. "*Purdue* must mean *rich*," I thought. The hall seemed bigger than our entire double-bricked school. Like the Harry Potter feast scenes, or Peter

Pan's imaginary banquet—that room became a blissful occasion for a naïve little guy in borrowed corduroys.

A few nights later, we gathered around our own tree pilfered from the local woods. Dad had managed a few generic presents, now wrapped in newsprint—but he missed their unwrapping and the miracle. The watering hole was open.

Someone knocked on our door, but when we opened it, nobody was there. Puzzled, we turned on the light . . . and there was the strangest thing—gifts and groceries covering the makeshift wooden plank sidewalk. They spilled onto the yard. I thought—"There really must be a Santa." Little did I know at the time that folks from the tiny local church (we didn't attend) had pulled the proverbial sleigh.

A few years ago, sitting in the far corner of that same Purdue Memorial Hall where this article began, my mind smiled for a while as I filled myself once again with a picturesque meal. Yes, that very room was a special place for a one-time "special" guest, and the site of a "happy thought" for life. But I began to get sentimental and tears flowed, realizing how blessed I had been then and now.

Just then, the plenary speaker paused. The stately Dr. John Gardner looked at the large Purdue crowd then added, "Please forgive my manners. You have a few guests here today from other universities. . . . . One special guest is Dr. Jerry Pattengale. He's one of the leading authorities on . . . ."

"Special guest" was about all that I heard. I was numb when he asked me to stand—wet-faced and deeply connected to my past.

Standing there in the corner of that great university hall that had seemed another world from Buck Creek, was, well, a salute to a Christmas past. A Buck Creek Christmas—and the power of education to transform one's opportunities and life contribution. After his speech, I left immediately to hide. I dried my face then darted to the nearest store and bought gifts for others' sidewalks.

During my return to Memorial Hall, John's words became a salute to teachers' past. To union wives' past. To anonymous neighbors and small churches. And to their successors—the keepers of Christmas present and the hope for special things to come.

Buck Creek Wisdom #17

"Apart from education and/or Christ, some people's lives will never change."

"Special guests are never self-appointed, and if so, we're all disappointed."

"Recognition is itself neutral unless respect is nearby."

"Being disillusioned is not a prerequisite for being disenfranchised, but barriers to the future often thwart hope for fulfillment."

Buck Creek & the Bible

There are many reasons that our nation emphasizes education, but it should always be about more than just a trade or skill. Our country's future depends on the other benefits of education—which some call "values," others "morals," and in some aspect many call it "civility." The Old Testament book of Proverbs is filled with wise sayings to help us live upright and healthier lives, such as, "Start children off on the way they should go, and even when they are old they will not turn from it." (Proverbs 22:6)

Dr. Jerry Pattengale

CHAPTER EIGHTEEN:
Don't Surprise Your Wife with an Ab Blaster

Buying my wife an "Ab Blaster" for Christmas had an adverse effect on New Year's resolutions.

This so-called revolutionary new help for stomach crunches caused me years of emotional pain.

My boys said the contraption was cool and argued that, "Mom will love it."

If love is measured by how quickly a gift can be tossed onto the porch, she adored it. She might as well have hit me with a frozen salmon and force-fed me Bob Dylan outtakes.

A decade later, that special gift has become legendary. When groups begin talking about bad gifts, my wife's story is the topper. She once pointed through the window to where her trophy landed.

No matter how naively we might intend gifts, any appearance of imposing a New Year's resolution on another doesn't work. The irony is that self-imposed resolutions usually fail as well—a lesson I first observed during my Buck Creek youth.

My aunts had resolved to lose weight on a revolutionary shaking machine. One of them would wrap a wide strap around her waist and then hit the power. What a jittering hoot.

The fat rolls vibrated, and with the strap it sort of looked like an attempt at lassoing Jell-O on a trampoline.

The idea behind the machine was that the motion was supposed to heat fat, causing it to disappear. However, the cause seemed to shake loose from effect.

This exercise machine, commonly called a vibrator belt, was the ultimate purchase for New Year's resolutions in the early 1970s. Along with the most recent Elvis album, my aunts seemed to have it all.

For months, they explained to friends how the machine worked, justifying their bizarre purchase.

Whenever such discussions began, we kids would scheme to snatch a view. We'd line vertically along the doorframe, swallowing our fist, trying not to laugh.

And sure enough, the vibrations started and *both* fists, to the elbows, weren't enough to stifle our snorts.

I don't recall my aunts ever breaking into a sweat, other than where that thick belt nearly disintegrated their skin.

The funniest thing was that they tended to be short, so after a few jiggles, the strap was less around their hips than around their heads. And in those days of teased hair, it was like watching Don King in a blender.

Like many New Year's gifts, those vibrator belts became coat hangers. And a few years later, unlike love handles, they disappeared.

The trouble with New Year's resolutions is that we tend to focus on weaknesses; on changing personal habits we think need attention.

Whether we try to impose resolutions on others or ourselves, focusing on strengths would likely produce resolutions that live longer and are more effective.

The Gallup organization recently released its robust Strengths Quest program, following the theory of focusing on the positives. It's helping more students finish college.

This type of "strengths approach" can also tie one's passion to a positive social change.

Willy Nelson's Farm Aid successfully combined his talent with crisis resolution. Jerry Lewis made the same commitment for muscular dystrophy research.

Their resolutions were principled more than personal, and outward looking instead of inward serving. These remarkable resolutions also had resilience amidst early resistance.

Kent Keith's *Anyway: The Paradoxical Commandments* is a little book that might help guide you in establishing principled resolutions.

He first published the list in a campus paper while a Harvard student. Thirty years later, he learned through a conference speaker that they had made their way to Mother Teresa's wall in Calcutta. He eventually published them anew:

People are illogical, unreasonable, and self-centered: Love them anyway.

If you do good, people will accuse you of selfish ulterior motives: Do good anyway.

If you are successful, you will win false friends and true enemies: Succeed anyway.

The good you do today will be forgotten tomorrow: Do good anyway.

Honesty and frankness make you vulnerable: Be honest and frank anyway.

The biggest men and women with the biggest ideas can be shot down by the smallest men and women with the smallest minds: Think big anyway.

People favor underdogs but follow top dogs: Fight for a few underdogs anyway.

What you spend years building may be destroyed overnight: Build anyway.

People really need help but may attack you if you do help them: Help people anyway.

Give the world the best you have and you'll get kicked in the teeth: Give the world the best you have anyway.

Years ago, I had the privilege of proofing some of Kent's forthcoming work—now easily located on the web.

Perhaps it would be in order to add a New Year's Paradoxical Commandment: "People may joke about your weight. Don't wait, hug them anyway." Also, you'll be happy to know that my wife gave her blessings for this column. That is, if I'd attempt to use her "Ab Blaster." Done.

Slipping on a shiny sweat suit about as old as the "Ab Blaster," I looked like a shrink-wrapped pear. I also noticed it's a lot easier to use the contraption while standing.

This year, I thought of something more practical. (I learned my lesson.) My gut reaction was to buy something for the house. I had seen one of these at many friends' homes, and thought it just might work.

It was a revolutionary coat hanger that's been on the market a few years. It's called Bowflex.

Buck Creek Wisdom #18

"A glimpse as a child can prompt a gaze as an adult."

"Exercise may be going in circles but it'll extend your world's rotations."

"Focusing on strengths likely produces healthy resolutions for perceived weakness."

Buck Creek & the Bible

After St. Paul warns of the consequences of living a sinful life (e.g., drunkenness, orgies and envy), he gives what is commonly called the "Fruit of Spirit." He says, "But the fruit of the Spirit is love, joy, peace, forbearance, kindness, goodness, faithfulness, gentleness and self-control." (Galatians 5:22) Regardless of our strengths and weakness, these are characteristics we should cherish in our lives and respect in others.

CHAPTER NINETEEN:
Deer on the Freeway

Imagine driving down the freeway and a man riding a huge deer passes by— holding on for dear life with a Bowie knife in his teeth! Those drivers witnessing this scene probably turned and said, "Now that's something you just don't see every day."

My cousin Danny recently shared, "To make matters worse, the thing took off against traffic!" He should know; he was on it. He nearly lost his life that day in 1972 on I-65 near Lafayette, IN, just a few miles from Buck Creek.

I had published over one hundred of my Buck Creek stories before discovering this amazing episode—and only learned of it after Danny read my article on our uncle falling from his tree stand on top of a deer. Reflecting on the fact that other hunters would ask our ill-fated uncle if he had his saddle ready for deer season, Danny nonchalantly added, "Well, Jerry Allen, of course you know about my deer jumping days." Seeing my puzzled look, he was tickled that such bizarre stories had escaped my notebooks.

Leaning against his cage of mammoth floppy-eared rabbits, right next to Bannie roosters that had been specially bred to have beard-like faces, he told me his stories—one old, one new.

On an otherwise routine day in 1972, Danny received a call from his friend—a policeman. A large deer had been struck on the freeway and was huddled near the road with a damaged leg. Not wanting to use a gun near the interstate and houses and fearful of the deer jumping in front of other cars, he called his avid hunting friend who lived nearby.

It's routine for hunters to use a knife to finish off a wounded deer, and there are ways to do so to cause the least amount of pain and trauma (as if being shot or hit by a car wasn't enough).

Hunters have their own euthanasia routines, and Danny's was simple: walk up on the blindside with a knife in his teeth, straddle it while hugging its neck and then puncture its lung. Well, all went well until the beast darted upwards, causing Danny to hold on with both arms and then ride like the wind.

"I thought I was gonna die. I could see cars coming at me . . . I couldn't let go long enough to grab the knife . . ." I asked, "Where was your brother Steve? What did you do?"

"Last I saw Steve he was rolling alongside the highway laughing his head off. . . . I painted a few cars that day." Seeing my puzzled face again, he clarified, "Pulling back as hard as I could on its neck, I slit its throat and the next thing I knew, the cars were all red." Afterward, Steve pulled up the truck; they threw the oversized deer in the back, and back to Buck Creek they went.

On a more recent occasion, Danny happened to be driving home when he heard a gunshot in the woods. Recognizing the truck on the wood's edge, he pulled over to see if his novice, hunting friend needed help. Eventually his friend exited the woods, but without the deer. The young hunter was unsure if he hit it, but "must not have." Being a religious follower of hunting rules, and concerned for a possible wounded deer, Danny had the careless hunter put his gun away because of the ensuing darkness, and go with him to look for "the huge buck" he said he missed. Not far into the woods they spotted a pool of blood and a little further found a large buck bedded beneath trees.

Danny took the lead, the deer didn't move (he assumed due to being shot), then proceeded to put it out of its misery. Instead, the alpha venison bucked him off, then rammed his friend into a tree and kept doing so. Danny managed to reach around a tree and grab both antlers while his friend escaped. "The dang thing kept ramming my hands against the tree, and finally my friend had enough sense to find my knife and stab him. . . and then the darndest thing—we realized we had the wrong deer." And Danny, the purist, used one of his hunting tags ". . .though they don't exactly have ones for knife season."

We see a lot of people doing bizarre things. Sometimes, they're obviously wrong—or are they? Danny regularly helps people and is highly respected in his county (he even purchased homes and cars for his four children for finishing school). It's easy to say, "Now that's something you just don't see every day."

It's always easy to jump erroneously from description to judgment. After all, we live in an era when millions bought tickets to see vacuous *Jackass* movies. But we need to remain a bit cautious, and the next time we hear someone say "Oh Dear . . ." pause a bit. You might start by asking, "Do you know Danny?"

While trying to help, sometimes we get hurt. While assisting others, we occasionally jeopardize ourselves. Other times, we simply need to wear "stupid" signs and move on down the highway.

Buck Creek Wisdom #19

"It's always easier to jump erroneously from description to judgment than to stand firmly on a proven foundation."

"There are times to ride boldly against traffic, and usually your own grip is your only safety belt."

"Before tackling a problem, make sure you're hitting the right object."

Buck Creek & the Bible

Although it would be a wakeup call to see a man riding a deer on the freeway, more unique events have occurred in history—miraculous but real. One of these is captured in the kids' song, "Joshua Fought the Battle of Jericho," which reflects the historic battle led by Moses's successor, Joshua. The recorded story outlines their march around the oasis city seven times, and then the walls collapsed. Although we can study archaeology and match the existence of an ancient city to that time and try to prove that walls indeed collapsed, at some point one either believes in the miraculous or does not. That God is supernatural and has power of this world. There is great promise for those who believe, as Joshua outlines shortly before crossing the Jordan for this legendary attack: "Be strong and very courageous. Be careful to obey all the law my servant Moses gave you [found in the first five books of the Old Testament]; do not turn from it to the right or to the left, that you may be successful wherever you go. Keep this Book of the Law always on your lips; meditate on it day and night, so that you may be careful to do everything written in it. Then you will be prosperous and successful. Have I not commanded you? Be strong and courageous. Do not be afraid; do not be discouraged, for the Lord your God will be with you wherever you go." (Joshua 1: 7-9)

Dr. Jerry Pattengale

CHAPTER TWENTY:
Dead Priests and Alive Issues

We had never met a Catholic in Buck Creek, and our non-religious relatives further distorted our views. They touted that "All Catholics are going to Hell," yet were clueless about how to get to heaven.

United Methodists were also suspect. Sometimes we stared at the Buck Creek steeple, ridiculing the unknown. Bizarre stories of cryptic rites surfaced fueling our paranoia.

From our schoolyard hill was a clear view of the simple-spired church on the opposing knoll. We second-graders found the whole religious world mysterious. Thousands of candles, draped coffins and dark eerie hallways certainly lurked behind the stained glass.

We had no idea that our Easter holiday had any connection to the whole affair.

"I bet that church is like one of those Catholic places," said dark-foggy-rimmed Denny, "like the one my relatives in Ohio visited."

Accusations abounded through teen years—swinging incense must be "of Satan." Worshipping the Pope was dating "the anti-Christ." And our good Hangman word, "indulgences," simply meant "paying off God."

85

"Those Catholics even think they drink real blood during communion. That's a God-ugly thought."

"God-ugly" . . . hm-m-m?

Perhaps we can all find uninformed views in our elementary and teen years. As we mature, knowledge should open our eyes. Proximity has a direct correlation to reducing paranoia.

I was in high school before understanding Communion and meeting a Catholic—my friend of thirty years, Tony Aretz (now president of Mt. St. Joseph's College).

Through the years I've dug for common ground between the Christian sects.

In the mid 1990s, my work took me deep within the bowels of an ancient church—the excavation of a fourth-century Coptic church in the remote desert of Wadi Natrun, Egypt.

We lived in the residence of the Coptic pope, His Holiness Pope Shenouda III. Near his monastic apartments, about halfway between Cairo and Alexandria, we unearthed remarkable remains.

In Indiana Jones fashion, my colleague descended with a miner's cap into a crypt-like chapel forty feet beneath the main floor, itself well below the desert surface.

Amidst scorpions, spiders, and "eight-step" vipers he entered a lost world of the *Hagia*—the holy ones.

He found a treasure of unique proportions—the only known painting of the early desert saints.

In a forgotten underground chamber in a lost church in remote Egypt, he was face to face with legendary saints.

These men were pillars of the Christian Church in Egypt, a contemporary movement to the early Catholic hierarchy in Rome.

In a sense, they were among the forefathers of all Christians—including the Protestants who came 1,100 years afterward and even distant Buck Creek adherents.

Somewhere in time, the desert Egyptian community had lost favor within society—likely during the Muslim invasions in the seventh century.

Next to the archaeological site is a wind-eroded mound encasing thousands of monks' graves with visible holy relics. Exposed skulls and other skeletal remains reminded us of the extent of their sacrifice and the leveling of time.

An irony surfaced—a little pot of gold coins, apparently dropped in flight and accidentally preserved in an upside down common clay container.

This find begged the question, "Why would a monk have a pot of gold in the desert?"

Perhaps like today, temptations had pricked at the hearts of a few. Or, more likely, it was their "Bread of the Poor" fund.

The gold cache was found against the backdrop of the holy hill of relics, a reminder of the sacrifice of thousands to live out their faith in an ascetic way.

These were truly holy people, saints worthy of veneration by modern Catholics, Copts and Protestants alike.

My work took me to another special religious site, this time in South Bend.

I attended early mass in the Crypt, a short walk above Notre Dame's grotto, with my friend Pat White (now president of Wabash College).

The service emphasized the universal nature of Christianity and Christ's appeal to all humankind, regardless of differences.

Both the informal and formal homilies highlighted the biblical call to cross secondary barriers and to celebrate what all Christians have in common—such as the Easter story.

I was a long way from gossipy Buck Creek recesses. Among the incense and icons in one of America's most esteemed Catholic churches, I was endorsing the plea for unity among Christians.

Then came the subtle reminder that not all has changed since my Buck Creek boyhood. The Crypt's service ended with communion, offered only to Catholic members.

As my colleague, a devout Catholic, stood with the majority of the crowd, we visiting Protestants remained seated—a manifestation of the awkward disconnect between the message and the moment. However, the difference was indeed momentary and mutually understood.

I recently interviewed a retired schoolteacher in Buck Creek, Peg Eckhart. She lives in a late-1800s quaint, soft-brick home adjacent to that spired church that had been as foreign to us as any crypt or abbey.

Intertwined throughout her scrapbook were links to that once mysterious church a few yards from her door.

This gracious woman's life was inextricably linked to the nearby pews. Without leaving her house, she provided my first look behind those once dark doors.

Knowledge, indeed, is our friend, and true friends help us to know.

And while not all priests and pastors have lived holy lives, they are outnumbered by centuries of saints buried in holy hills.

At the least, the Easter story should unite those who call themselves Christian and prompt grace to those who don't.

Buck Creek Wisdom #20

"Proximity has a direct correlation to reducing paranoia."

"Suspect teachings are usually manifest in awkward disconnects between the message and the moment."

"The Christian story has many chapters but one thesis: Jesus died once so we don't have to die twice."

Buck Creek & the Bible

Since the time of Christ and the Apostles, the Church has taken many forms. It has included many branches (e.g., Catholic, Protestant, Eastern Orthodox, Coptic), denominations (e.g., Baptists, Methodists, Presbyterians), and further sub-splits (e.g., Free Methodists, United Methodists and Wesleyans). Even while the New Testament was being written, there were differences about both practice and teachings—but the writers were clear to define orthodox teaching. Also, St. Paul reminds us that within the Church (and now we would say, regardless of which denomination we choose for association) we are "one body," and have our role for Christ's purpose. "Just as a body, though one, has many parts, but all its many parts form one body, so it is with Christ. For we were all baptized by one Spirit so as to form one body—whether Jews or Gentiles, slave or free—and we were all given the one Spirit to drink. Even so the body is not made up of one part but of many." (1 Corinthians 12: 12-14)

CHAPTER TWENTY-ONE:
Hunting Deer with a Musket

He pulled the musket's trigger and "BOOM!" But the buck standing only twenty yards away looked up and seemed to say, "You idiot." My relative yelled, "Why aren't you falling? You've been shot. What's wrong with you? Fall!" His hunting buddy laughed loudly as the deer ran away, then blurted, "You forgot to pack the paper cartridge. The lead ball just rolled down the end of your barrel!"

He forgot some of the basics; it had been twenty years since he last shot a musket.

And with self-effacing laughter, after telling me this story he added, "Last week during rifle season, another big deer walked slowly in front of me. BOOM! It also just ran away. The bullet hit a little tree, dead center—it was only two inches wide, and I nailed it! The only tree in the whole #$@*! field, and I hit it!"

If you've hunted, you have your stories.

Roger, a sixty-five-year-old friend in Michigan, had his climbing belt snap while shimmying up a tree to reach his stand. He hung upside down by his boots after being knocked out—the back of his head slammed the tree. "Nearly died there with my boot spikes stuck in the tree." He and his son had hunted together for thirty years, but they had forgotten to check their equipment. "Oh, my son was snuggled in his deer blind just out of sight through the woods." I wonder what the deer thought as they saw Roger hanging there.

I've also wondered what the deer in Buck Creek thought as my uncle writhed in pain with broken ribs after falling onto the deer's back? Or about my brother's beef jerky scentand Twinkie wrapper noises that warned deer for miles that hunters were in their woods.

These aren't stupid people. The musket mishap happened to a brilliant engineer and owner of a successful tool and die company in Ohio. The unconscious upside down hunter had an earned Ph.D., is highly respected in his county, and hunted religiously for decades. My brother graduated from high school at fifteen. My uncle who fell on the deer, well . . . that might be a different story.

We can buy insurance for some things that happen to smart people, and even to those of us less endowed, but the truth is there is no assurance that we'll not find ourselves the victim of our own lapse of judgment.

While we might forget some basics from our childhood that ruin our best intentions, there are basics much more serious than forgetting to pack gunpowder in a recreational musket. We might lose our balance and fall at times—causing much more serious damage than breaking ribs before an audience of giggling venison. Some forgotten basics can lead to mistakes that can knock us out for a while, stealing our reputation, and no one laughs.

But the deepest regrets are when people remember the basics and ignore them. Howard Stern ridicules basic human decency. Governor Rod Blagojevich ignored basic integrity when he allegedly tried to sell President Obama's Senate seat. Bernard Madoff bilked investors of fifty billion dollars when he misrepresented the basics of private property. ACORN workers funded prostitution and ignored the very basics of human dignity that once underpinned their organization.

We'll never be able to stop all unethical or immoral decisions—we humans are a fallen lot with a bent toward sinning. I'm tipping my worldview here, one that endorses the concept of a supreme being that has absolute standards and instills within us with a sense of oughtness. There is a common notion that some things are right, some are pure. There is an inherent sense of decency.

Regardless of our spiritual and philosophical beliefs, there remains hope that education can help thwart decisions intentionally harmful to others. That lists of values, like those of Aquinas, frame responses. That our conscience is attached to consequences. That the liberal arts can help future leaders understand economic justice, humanitarian standards, and the strengths and weaknesses of the human condition. And that through all of our learning and refining of rational thought, not to dismiss as whimsical comments like Brit Hume's that remind us of our finiteness and the likelihood of forces greater than ourselves.

And speaking of miracles, I'm not sure my engineer relative will manage to get a deer anytime soon without special help. As irony would have it, while leaving his cabin recently an entire herd just stared at us as we drove away, and three of them played dodge with our car. I wondered if the big buck standing off to the side was laughing, knowing we had just left the cabin of the legendary musket hunter.

Buck Creek Wisdom #21

"Don't be surprised when consequences are linked to your conscience."

"Although there's an inherent sense of decency within each of us, there's also an apparent sense of decadence around all of us."

"We often miss targets before we ever take aim."

Buck Creek & the Bible

St. Paul stresses the role of our conscience, a God-given barometer for decisions, but doesn't set it as the final standard: "My conscience is clear, but that does not make me innocent. It is the Lord who judges me." (1 Corinthians 4:4)

Dr. Jerry Pattengale

CHAPTER TWENTY-TWO:
Reality TV Super-Sized Me

It was Reality TV—a super-sized me. I sat before millions in a shirt that made me look like an awning advertisement.

Before appearing on that national TV show, I joked to the makeup artist – "I only ask that you make me look like Robert Redford."

A few minutes later my extra pounds pounded across the airwaves. Instead of Redford they saw Humpty. Instead of high society, they got a guest in need of a corset.

While a former beauty star was asking me about "purpose-guided education," a topic of important substance, I wanted to guide this *Bloomin' Onion One* offstage. TV transformed my belt into a black rubber band around a 100% cotton balloon.

The sofa nearly imploded under my weight—wedging knees and belly together. Friction from my heavy breathing could have sparked a fire.

While she read the teleprompter, I leaned a throw pillow against my side—but needed a futon.

The close-up of the host showed her perfect face and chin. Oh no! It switched to me. I had so many chins I needed a bookmarker to track my lips. And I suddenly noticed more moles and bumps than my barnyard. My lobes could have passed for Dumbo's.

My physique jumped out like a lemming with a life jacket. The host and I were as different as *Napoleon Dynamite* and *Les Miserable*, smashed tater tots on silk.

I had prepared for the interview. I knew my material well, like the back of my hand—then, "Oh rats, I never noticed those homely fingernails." The interview ended and within minutes I was rolled offstage to recover from my self-imposed, self-esteem journey. The pixels were filled with Pattengale, and it wasn't pretty.

It dawned on me later that I hadn't worried about appearance until going to make-up. Like most days, I probably hadn't combed my hair. I had the funeral-ironed shirt—that is, the front was pressed while the back sported a topographical map look. I'm now over 50, and my mind is usually not on appearance. Blue or black socks—who cares? Who I am is more about . . . well . . . the big screen thrust reality upon me.

And that is what's transpiring with regularity on TV—Reality shows. Listen forward a few years:

"Mommy, why do I have a hooked nose and a snaggletooth smile—and you don't?" She replied, "Well son, I was on *Extreme Makeover* before you were born."

"But you always tell me I'm beautiful. Does that mean you changed your looks to be ugly?"

I suppose it's not too much of a stretch to assume that such conversations will occur in a few years as Extreme Makeover guests and NipTuck fans begin to deal with curious children.

And what of family reunions? Imagine years of looking like everyone else with hooked-noses and snaggletooth smiles, and suddenly a cousin falls into the party like a leaf from another's family tree. White capped teeth that would make Donny Osmond jealous. A nose from the Brad Pitt line. A Redford chin. A Brittney Spears belly. It's all possible.

The public irony is our outcry against baseball's *Balko* and rampant steroids while applauding outrageous makeover surgery. At what point does correcting a facial deformity disrupt genuine characteristics? To fix disruptive features ("deformities") seems far afield from forged beauty.

Imagine Barbara Streisand with a Hepburn nose. Think of a gapless David Letterman smile. Marty Feldman with Jim Caviezel eyes. A silk-skinned James Olmos. And picture *The Office* and *Whose Line Is It Anyway?* with made over regulars. Steve Carrel, Drew Carey and Colin Mochrie have Norman Rockwell appeal—they're believable, genuinely unique. The show's reruns would become *Who Cares, Anyway?* Likewise, Humphrey Bogart is no Elvis, but that's why we know them both.

After my TV broadcast, relatives called. They didn't mention the puffy part. They didn't notice the moles, the long earlobes and pronounced nose. They saw the same kid who chased pigs through Buck Creek fields, who waded Sugar Creek with a Zebco 202, who dropped silver roof paint on Grandma's flowers, and who played basketball on a dirt court with a worn ball. Older, somewhat weathered, but the same kid. To them, I'm still Jerry Allen. They helped me to learn early that *if you try to make an impression, that's the impression you'll make.*

In some ways, education and jobs separated our worlds. But we still look the same, like the beaches at the end of *The Sneetches*. I'll likely need a contoured wooden coffin lid for my nose—but it'll be hewn from our family tree.

I love those Buck Creek people. They're my people. With distinguished noses, round chins, plump figures. My grandpa died recently and lived nearly a century. He walked closer to the ground with each passing year. He worked until ninety, and our biggest worry wasn't his heart but tripping over his earlobes. But if you line up humanity across the globe—he'd be a top pick among wonderful people, and very top among grandpas. All of him makes the man—and I love that man unaltered.

Yes, the reality of TV helped me to see that my weight is a health issue, and I've actually eaten more salads since then. But my double chins, bumps, big nose, short legs, pencil lips and generic hips—that's me. That's reality. The key isn't making surface changes to be attractive, but attracting attention to changes of substance.

Buck Creek Wisdom #22

"If you try to make an impression, that's the impression you'll make."

"First impressions are never secondary; entry is ten times easier than re-entry."

"The key isn't making surface changes to be attractive, but attracting attention to changes of substance."

Buck Creek & the Bible

"Your beauty should not come from outward adornment, such as elaborate hairstyles and the wearing of gold jewelry or fine clothes. Rather, it should be that of your inner self, the unfading beauty of a gentle and quiet spirit, which is of great worth in God's sight." (1 Peter 3:3-4) These verses have been interpreted in many ways, with some religious movements restricting the use of jewelry and fine apparel. The historic context is advice for women in the first century, but its underlying principle transcends the ages for all of us. It's not about what we can't do, or can't wear, but about our "inner self" or pure heart and disposition before God.

CHAPTER TWENTY-THREE:
My Neighbor Punched James Dean

My neighbor punched James Dean.
Harold at six-four couldn't take the little gadfly anymore.
"He just kept pestering me, and I kept warning him," recounts Harold. "I warned him, 'Now Jimmy, if you don't quit I'm going to have to hit you.' He didn't stop, and so I punched him in the stomach."

The fun-loving retired Harold continues, "After I hit him, Jimmy bent over, then said, 'Harold, that was a good one.'" Harold laughs when asked to retell the story about "Little Jimmy," a "piece of work."

Jimmy, according to my neighbor with his whole history within ten miles of Dean's Fairmount, Indiana home, "was just one of the boys" but "was always up to something—always full of energy."

During the fall of 1948, Harold and Fairmount High had no idea that the wiry, bent-over, flat-topped, horn-rimmed boy would one day be its legendary full-headed alum. And James Dean, though full of life and adventure, didn't know that the fist that hit him would farm for sixty years after his own body would be placed six feet under.

James Dean left his Fairmount farm and traveled the country. Harold has rarely left the county.

James became a familiar face to millions. Harold needs an ID at local stores.

James Dean lived on the edge and wanted to plow new ground. Harold plowed the same ground into his seventies.

James would become a heartthrob for masses of young women. Harold was likely a looker in his day, but chose to spend the last sixty years with magnetic Marcella—the unofficial queen of our country parts.

James would become identified with a red Porsche Spider. Harold can be found in a four-door faded-blue Bonneville with over 200,000 miles.

James wore jeans and a t-shirt with his hallmark cigarette dangling from his lip. You might catch Harold in a t-shirt, but not to show off his physique—rather, to cool down after mowing. Being cool takes priority over looking cool.

James would provide the motivation of thousands of Mercury owners to drive their classics to Fairmount. Harold's home draws a few cars a year, usually for strawberries, hay or a tool or two.

James pursued Hollywood and found it. Harold pursued heaven and will never lose it.

James spawned posters and neon signs. Harold Mart, like myself, isn't exactly poster material. And, Wal-*Mart* and K-*Mart* signs aren't referring to my neighbor.

James would become the "Rebel without a Cause." Harold would become Harold.

A few years ago, Harold and Marcella sold their 500-acre farm—their only means of subsistence. They still have a few leaning barns and a house Harold helped his father build from native timbers.

Their lives haven't seen stage lights, but rather heat bulbs in sub-zero weather in hog barns. They haven't had the luxury of racecars, but they've experienced the joy of new tractor tires on their off-brand Oliver. They're more familiar with *Ball* jars and ball joints than bars and ballrooms.

James Dean set his eyes on the Pacific and headed west. Harold and Marcella have gone west for the winter, oh, about five miles to Hackleman for annual mower repairs at Drucks' Snapper dealer.

James and Harold took divergent paths from the Fairmount halls, and both of their lives draw our attention. Dean's adventure and risk perks our ears and resonates with our curiosity. The stable surefootedness of a lifetime farmer appeals to our need for security and roots.

I recently visited my little hometown of Buck Creek, less than an hour's drive west from Dean's tombstone. Unlike Fairmount, there are no legendary names or stories of Hollywood adventure—and no celebrity cause saved the high school. However, there are Harolds, plenty of them, who have maintained their farms and livelihood within a few miles of their childhood homes. And each of them likely knows the story of James Dean—the life of adventure and fun. The life of risk—throwing caution to the wind.

Unlike Buck Creek, Fairmount's old brick high school stood decades longer. Not because it's where Harold went. Not because it has a daily function in the community. Not because it's a priceless piece of architecture. Rather, because it's the school where James went, where the common kid from a common town established a common background to contrast his celebrity rise. When he died in 1955, Fairmount was born in the world's eyes.

Harold, who devoted his entire life to a rather focused cause, has fond memories of the high school, even encounters with Dean, a mediocre athlete—now the embodiment of independent confidence.

Most counties have their Harolds, but the entire country shares one James Dean. Otherwise, we'd be all too familiar with wondering, aimless, carefree adventurers. Imagine if our community were all Deans and only one Harold. We'd have fewer if any farms, and want ads for responsible citizens to run for office and to teach our children.

James allows us to have wild dreams. Harold helps us to see the reality of responsibility. James appeals to youthful desires, Harold to the desire to help our youth.

There's a postscript to this story. A few years ago, I was the guest speaker at Fairmount's "Legends Diner" on Main Street—there to read from these Buck Creek stories (familiar to them through newsprint) and to provide a motivational challenge to an older group, nearly all contemporaries of James Dean. It was a memorable moment—a crowded back room clothed in James Dean wallpaper and historic Dean pictures. And, sitting head and shoulders above the crowd was seventy-one-year-old Harold Mart. While reading about the contrasts, we all laughed at times; then, fighting tears, we realized the measure of the man next to us.

Afterward, Harold, humble through it all, asked my wife and me to go for a ride. Not far north of Fairmount he pulled into the cemetery and drove us to Dean's graveside. "Jimmy was a good boy," said Harold. "I thought you'd like to see his stone." And then in one of those most precious of moments, he pointed just above James' simple pinkish stone, east a hundred feet or so, to two simple but darker grave markers, both reading "Mart." Harold purchased them thirty years ago to ensure a local and debt-free resting place—another contrast between the Fairmount phenomenon and tall farmer.

As we drove away, Harold pointed out the striking signature farm where Dean worked, and then throughout the countryside, he pointed to many places where homes of friends once stood and where memories still lived. Then it hit me anew, that the same giant of a teen who hit James Dean had hit me. The fist of his life connected solidly deep within me. "Harold, that was a good one."

The life of a James Dean is fascinating. That of a Harold is motivating.

Buck Creek Wisdom #23

"True character stands the test of time, and the grading scale rarely changes."

"Being cool takes priority over looking cool."

"James Dean Principle: A rebel without a cause gives little cause for rebellion and much for reflection."

Buck Creek & the Bible

A constant theme in the Bible is patience. Sometimes it's a reminder of our personal virtue for its inherent value: "A person's wisdom yields patience; it is to one's glory to overlook an offense."(Proverbs 19:11) Other times it's for practical reasons: "Through patience a ruler can be persuaded, and a gentle tongue can break a bone." (Proverbs 25:15) "The end of a matter is better than its beginning, and patience is better than pride." (Ecclesiastes 7:8)

Dr. Jerry Pattengale

CHAPTER TWENTY-FOUR:
I Wore a Scarlet Letter to College

My college professor listened to my answer then looked at me funny—probably searching for a lobotomy scar.

For me "SAT" was a capitalized past tense of "sit." The "classics" were vintage Mopars and Mustangs. Serious reading was *Field & Stream*.

My jacked-up Gremlin with its fifteen-foot CB whip antenna, oversized chrome wheels and Roy Clark eight-tracks represented priorities—and none implied academics.

Yep, I entered college with a big scarlet "A" on my chest for "*At-risk* of failing college." The diagnosis was correct by educational standards, but the prognosis was suspect.

A Sierra Club member at a George Bush rally would have been less conspicuous. I was given about as much chance to succeed as The Heritage Foundation erecting a Ted Kennedy statue.

They tagged me as "Economically at-risk," even though I had learned to improvise. I once took a college date bowling on the courthouse sidewalk with a borrowed ball and ten spray cans. (Okay, I admit—repeat dates were rare).

In my hometown of Buck Creek, "life skills" weren't learned in remedial classes. Rather, they were developed while fishing with a broken, drag-less Zebco 202 reel and landing an eighteen-inch, six-pound small-mouth bass on a two-pound line then embellishing the account at the smoke-filled Americus Restaurant while deep-frying catfish. Creativity 101, Math 101 and Communication 101 all in one.

In Buck Creek, "study skills" meant scouting deer paths or learning *Bondo*™ techniques for ill-designed Suburban fenders.

"Critical thinking skills" weren't learned through abstract Venn diagrams. Rather, through critiquing welding beads on stock car frames and strategizing Euchre moves at family hog roasts.

The "First-generation" label never resonated. Although my parents quit school shortly after junior high, I asked, "Why does that matter?"

However, the "Under-represented" tag made sense, but seemed to omit Buck Creek "hicks." Shaggy-headed, night crawler-hunting, overhaul-wearing, Sassafras-drinking, uninsured demolition derby fans were rare on campus—but "statistically insignificant."

"Student Orientation Weekend" made sense for this multi-tagged "at-risk" student—after all, the acronym spelled "SOW." Coming from poverty, the weekend was more a cultural than communal adjustment.

The above "at-risk" tags are important but miss an overriding positive. As a sixteen-year-old high school graduate I had a fire in my belly, a "purpose"—a deep disagreement with some political decisions and an interest in the health and collapse of societies. I had a desire to make a difference. A Harrison High School teacher, Dr. Brewer, had prompted me to engage primary questions. Like Plato's "Allegory of the Cave," I had seen the light and became unsettled with some social solutions. I couldn't articulate my purpose, and needed a firm knowledge base—but I should have had a full-body sign to eclipse the rest, one with a big "IM" for "intrinsic motivation."

When the college recruiter began calling, it wasn't the college's name, faculty, or facilities that got my attention. Rather, it was my unarticulated desire to learn more—to discover and to articulate better answers. And, the school offered me a place to live—free.

The John N. Gardner Institute for Excellence in Undergraduate Education (Brevard, NC) developed Foundations for Excellence in the First College Year—which assesses the health of colleges' initial experiences. It could likely supplant dependence on the problematic for-profit ratings in popular magazines, such as *U.S. News & World Report* and *Peterson's*. *Foundations* is interested in Scarlet Letters and for good reasons—some labels belong on the institution rather than the individual. IUPU (in Indianapolis) and Indiana Wesleyan University were among the twenty-four schools selected nationally as Foundational Institutions.

While for-profit ratings of colleges will continue to provide helpful data on the overall health of institutions, *Foundations for Excellence* will provide a non-profit organization's assessment of that important first-year. *U.S. News* might indicate large library holdings and alumni giving, but it won't tell you much about the important first year—when the largest attrition (leaving college) takes place.

Whether or not a school has four-year graduation rates above the national average of 32%, keep in mind that most colleges lose the largest percentage of "unsuccessful" students during the first year.

By the way, that fire in my belly back in 1975 is better understood today, both personally and professionally. One of the *Foundations'* standards being used to evaluate the nation's colleges is called "Life Purpose." That is, the intentional involvement of *"all students in an exploration of their life purpose . . ."* It's an assessment of the process from values clarification to intrinsic motivation—a key to student success. Indiana Wesleyan University and Indiana University released a study on this standard to a conference in Southampton, England (me, Ed St. John, Bill Millard, Brad Garner and others). Its startling figures affirm the focus on "purpose" in a curriculum (at IWU) that assists an astoundingly higher percentage of students to graduate. From 2.36% to 12% more students in the various groups graduated (1700 total students in the four-year study). This project was part of the Lumina Foundation-sponsored "Indiana Project for Academic Success," and it builds on a decade of work supported by the Lilly Endowment.

Research reveals that in 1975 I either wore the wrong Scarlet Letter, or I wore the institution's by mistake. Yes, I was at-risk in the standard categories, but not in the one that mattered most—*a sense of purpose*. The common thread reaching from the 1970s to the present is that labels are still used. Fortunately, new tailors aren't forgetting the institutions and the intrinsic dynamic of the human condition.

Buck Creek Wisdom #24

"An institution is a systematic response to a recurring need, and unchecked recurring needs in societies nullify the likelihood of healthy institutions."

"The person most likely to experience a fulfilling life is the one with an overriding sense of life purpose."

"Scarlet Letters reflect more about the giver than the receiver."

"We categorize life for convenience; we label people for correction."

Buck Creek & the Bible

For people of faith, they often find a sense of purpose aligned with their religion. For Christians, their fulfillment often comes from contributing to the cause of their church and committing to some aspect of what God has called them to. They also find strength in the Bible's promises for this journey: "But those who hope in the Lord will renew their strength. They will soar on wings like eagles; they will run and not grow weary, they will walk and not be faint." (Isaiah 40:31)

Dr. Jerry Pattengale

CHAPTER TWENTY-FIVE:
Pigs on Roof: A Buck Creek Reflection on Faith-Based Initiatives

Dad was unemployed but brought home the bacon—five dead pigs strapped to our VW bug.

The car's silhouette against the winter night looked like Don King in a hair net. Ropes, borrowed wire and battery cables held the hairy hams in place. With the front trunk ajar, the sow chauffeuring spectacle had sauntered home.

A semi had overturned a few miles from our Buck Creek neighborhood and its hoofed cargo scattered across the Indiana highway, Route 25. Swine everywhere. Some dead. Some injured. All free for the taking and dad took freely; he made a haul, literally. Our little white car was covered with "the other white meat." We weren't just viewing gnarly beasts in sun tanning positions—we were looking at weeks of meals.

We had one large dull knife and carpentry tools. After draping plastic around the kitchen, Mom beat the pork chops out of those lifeless carcasses. The evening was surrealistic. The sinister smiles on those pigs matched Dad's. Happy with joy and cheap beer, he celebrated his timely treasure.

At school we were reading *Animal Farm*, and it was difficult not to envision Napoleon smiling on our kitchen table. Eating any meal at home without seeing pinkish lipless grins was a challenge.

While most kids were either watching Bonanza or doing homework, we were making our own Rawhide. School progressed the next day in a daze.

I had just experienced a sleepless, family-generated, rated-R evening and was supposed to fit into the normal school routine. It wasn't the last time I'd look around and wish for a "free pass" for the day. Wish somehow to plant my foot and stop the world's spin and time itself. Wish somehow to catch up to normalcy.

A few years ago, over thirty years after the pigs on the roof, I found myself staring at another table covered with meat—at Ceiba's Restaurant in Washington D.C. This time, ham had fancy names with ornate garnishes and microscopic vegetables. The Epicurean menus didn't come with a VW emblem.

I was there for meetings with the White House Faith-Based Initiatives (since renamed under President Obama), and realized on several occasions the link to the Department of Education's "No Child Left Behind" efforts, an agency with its own faith-based center (www.fbci.gov).

President Bush joined the meetings and set the tone with some key phrases that resonated with the diverse Hilton crowd and with my own Buck Creek journey. His truths matched my reality. He noted that, "government can pass laws and hand out money, but it cannot hand out love."

Not long after the pig butchering incident, my mother finally left Buck Creek and my largely absent father. And, without many options, she left us five older kids to find a place to live while she moved west with our three younger brothers. At sixteen, a Wesleyan pastor took me in (Rev. Richard Cowley). Though I was longhaired and un-churched, his faith prompted him to hand out love.

President Bush also noted that it is, "important to the future of America to promote ownership." He reminded us that, "all the documents in trying to buy a home makes some people nervous. It makes me nervous—I'm in temporary housing." We all laughed: Democrats, Republicans and Libertarians, the Catholic father next to me, and the rabbis nearby. Handing out love struck a cord, and so did his gesture at identifying with paperwork.

As a teen, new friends at my adopted home (the friendly little Wesleyan church in Lafayette, Indiana), helped me navigate a stack of federal financial aid forms (FAFSA). I had graduated young and suddenly had an interest in college—and in the "free" housing and food that came with it. Pell grants paved the way for this Buck Creek boy, and a faith-based group led me to that federal path. It took both.

Whether faith-based or not, the President reminded us that, "a life of personal responsibility is a life of fulfillment." And that we, collectively as a society and individually as funders, need to support groups that help people toward that end, faith-based or not. "It's hard to be a results-oriented society if we don't focus on results," George W. noted and challenged us to support sensible initiatives that showed results. "Faith-based organizations provide models of success."

He encouraged the foundation and corporate leaders present to remove barriers to faith-based programs—noting that of 50 large foundations surveyed, 1/5 prohibited faith-based funding . . . [and out of] 20 of the largest corporations, only 6% of giving went to faith-based organizations. However, there was some positive news among federal funding—approximately 2.1 billion dollars went to faith-based organizations, around a 7% increase since this initiative began.

This issue transcends political leanings—the national faith-based director at the time, Jim Towey, was a Democrat and high profile lawyer (including Mother Teresa's). I suppose half or more of the Hilton crowd were Democrats as well. My later trip to the White House saw Jay Hein in charge of Towey's former office, and one where principles drove politics, not vice versa. Dr. Hein (now president of the Sagamore Institute) continues to make decisions on principles not politics.

As a sixteen-year-old graduate without a home, I had no idea of the kind pastor's politics, and still don't. I only know that his family showed me love and made sure I wasn't left behind. As I listened to our President from a few yards away, I found him believable. Though he lacked the eloquence of a Reagan or Clinton, I sensed a concern that would have placed President Bush at the table with my mother chopping meat to feed our family. I sensed a person that for no political attention would have paused to ask me where I was heading with my garbage bag luggage at such a young age. In many ways, if we are going to ensure that no child is left behind hungry or disenfranchised, we need to leave our politics behind.

Perhaps the President's most profound statement, though intended as humor, was about Jim Towey's amazing career profile. "I always wondered what kind of a society we live in that Mother Teresa needed a lawyer."

Thanks to the merging of faith-based and fund-based programs—an unofficial merger that helped to end my dining from overturned semis—generations of hungry kids will find a place at the higher educational table.

Buck Creek Wisdom #25

"It's an indictment on the human condition that Mother Teresa needed a lawyer."

"We need to make decisions on principles not politics."

"Bringing home the bacon takes many forms, and so does the bacon."

Buck Creek & the Bible

"Religion that God our Father accepts as pure and faultless is this: to look after orphans and widows in their distress and to keep oneself from being polluted by the world." (James 1:27)

CHAPTER TWENTY-SIX:
Dynamite and Explosive Ideologies

By age nineteen, I had seen explosives intended to topple a presidency and others used to build dreams.

From my Jerusalem dorm room, I could hear the faint echoes of bombing near the Golan Heights. It was 1977, a few days before Egyptian President Anwar Sadat's visit.

On the eve of this controversial trip, all was calm. Too calm. A rifle shot pierced the silent night and screamed the length of the Hinnom Valley beneath my window.

In a cold sweat on a stuffy night, fear supplanted sleep.

Henry Kissinger's bulletproof car was imported to shuttle Sadat past the Old City, across the valley, and then up the other side to the Knesset, Israel's Capitol Hill.

Sadat arrived amidst great anticipation and tension. The Islamic world was divided over a Muslim leader visiting Jews.

After praying at the Al-Aqsa mosque, Sadat's motorcade navigated streets intended for chariots, not black sedans.

My unabated view from atop the crenellated Turkish walls remains vivid thirty-five years later, a clear view of the Jewish hurt locker squad.

His car was about to exit the King David Gate, turn left, and cross the valley to return to the New City (modern Jerusalem). The parade following his entourage was unaware that soldiers were diffusing a bomb found moments earlier beneath the lone bridge.

Muslim fundamentalists had intended to assassinate President Sadat. Some on both sides didn't want the gap bridged between Muslims and Jews (Islamic fundamentalists would succeed in ending his life in Egypt four years later).

The last time I had seen explosives was in Buck Creek, and they, too, were used on a road—but to build it.

My family lived in the country, northwest of town. We had to drive through the creek to reach our land—that is, until my dad and uncles cleared a road over the hill for a new entrance.

The Pattengale men blasted tree stumps from the hillside. I raced from our snub-nosed bus many afternoons to watch the explosions and to help auger holes beneath the stumps.

My brothers, cousin Johnny and I took shelter as a lone stick of dynamite would dislodge mammoth obstacles. Occasionally, a Sassafras tree exploded and the fragrance sweetened the air. We horded the shredded roots and for months dipped precious tea from a stovetop cauldron.

A few times, the blasting was close to our makeshift house. Uncle Bill parked his old Chevy Impala next to the stumps with the windows rolled down and plywood covering the tires.

On cue, the dynamite sent roots, stones and dirt flying. The side of the car lifted. The back slid a bit. His plan worked; few pieces sprayed our house's mismatched metal siding.

We ran through the lingering smoke to see the new dents. At day's end, we'd clean the debris from Uncle Bill's car for a quarter.

He grabbed a longneck bottle of Falls City from my dad's cooler, propped it between his legs, lit up a filterless Camel and drove through the creek and onto the gravel road that eventually led him home.

For tougher trees, two or three sticks were used. Real fireworks ensued.

Mom often warned of dynamite's danger, even the power of the little bullet-size blasting cap. And when fuses sparkled, my uncles ran for cover. We kids were further off but felt too close.

Although the danger excited us, the explosive power enlightened us.

In the end, the dynamite saved hundreds of hours of work. It's hard to imagine dislodging those hillside trees without it.

Perhaps that's what the Muslim radicals thought when they planted the bomb beneath the bridge. If the cause was worthy enough, the means was tolerable.

Ideological differences, as goes this suspect rationale, are settled through elimination of the opposing ideologue. And, goes the strategy: explosives expedite outcomes.

Although still a teenager, I realized that the problem wasn't the explosive. It could also be used to exert power for constructive purposes.

Rather, the problem was an explosive ideology.

Socrates said that people performing evil acts are simply acting in ignorance; they're uneducated.

History has proven him wrong on this score. Westerners too often see the routine terrorist attacks in the Middle East as uncivil actions by uneducated people.

While "uncivil" is usually appropriate, "uneducated" is a misnomer.

An educational journey should help the learner to differentiate between ignoble and noble causes and to identify values beneath those causes. Bill Bennett's recent *America* history series offers this approach (Thomas Nelson), as do my recent student success books (McGraw-Hill). I heard this former Secretary of Education (3/25/2010) pause before an engaged Sagamore Institute crowd and thank three of the Navajo Code Talkers (present) for helping to save America—what Lincoln considered "the last best hope of earth."

Westerners are growing increasingly afraid to discuss values—an alarming development.

A few days after Sadat left Jerusalem, an elderly woman handed foreign college students entering the Old City a package to deliver, playing on her difficulty to make the trip. While they stopped to shop a bit in the Old City, the package exploded, mangling the shop and one of the students.

Above the store was an elementary school, and many of its kids were seriously wounded; a couple died.

I don't recall if the children were Muslim or Jewish, only their dismembered bloody bodies.

Innocence shredded. Mothers wailing. Fathers screaming. Teachers stunned. Innocence gone.

One set of values protects innocent life. Another takes it.

At some point, education is all about values though authors like Stanley Fish ardently disagree and write pieces entitled "Save the World on Your Own Time." Stanley Hauerwas and others offer strong responses to Fish (see *Debating Moral Education*, 2010).

My hope is that liberally educated people have a common notion of civility, that students learn that some ideological values are contradictory—and the law of non-contradiction states that both can't be correct. That blowing up healthy bridges is rarely ever civil, and the intentional killing of children is more than anti-American, it's reprobate in any moral language.

Buck Creek Wisdom #26

"Explosive ideologies tend to shred lives."

"Education not distinguishing between noble and ignoble notions needs schooling."

"We often don't miss the shade until we dislodge deep roots."

Buck Creek & the Bible

Christians have rather diverse interpretations on fighting and going to war. What is clear is that there are times when you can choose to show grace and mercy to your foes and other times when survival is at stake. In the former situation: "If your enemy is hungry, give him food to eat; if he is thirsty, give him water to drink. In doing this, you will heap burning coals on his head, and the Lord will reward you." (Proverbs 25:21) When survival is involved, "I keep my eyes always on the Lord. With him at my right hand, I will not be shaken." (Psalm 16:8)

Dr. Jerry Pattengale

CHAPTER TWENTY-SEVEN:
When Old Women Speak - The Easter Chicken

When my ninety-year-old Grandma Kaufman showed up at her neighbor's bonfire with a bucket of water, it was obvious she didn't like the rock 'n' roll music. When she threw the water on the party's host, it was obvious she liked her even less.

"The music was too loud, Jerry Allen, too loud. Devil's music! Communists!!... I warned her, my neighbor's girl…so ya know what I did? I took a pail of water over. She argues with me. Ya know what I did, Jerry Allen? I looked at the fire, looked at the water, then I threw it on her!" A fiery pride filled Grandma's eyes while I bit my lip. She rubbed her sandpaper hands together and her eyes glimmered.

We could laugh about her disposition. Any new neighbor became a bad one. The fault, always theirs, and vengeance, always hers. Two years after the bonfire incident her generic white hen came up missing. "Jerry Allen, I knew those neighbors—ya know, the evil ones with the chicken farm—they stole her. They stole her, Jerry Allen, the same way they gots so many others over ther." Rubbing her hands together, "Ya know what I did, Jerry Allen?!...Real early one morning I got her back. I sure did! I marched right over yonder, opened the gate until they all ran free [hundreds of generic white chickens]. And there she was—Henrietta, my hen. I told ya they was evil! And I told 'em so, too!"

That day hundreds of white hens ran through the streets—Christmas for some folks. And there in her tiny house she likely kept rubbing those hands together while some frightened hen in her living room had no idea why she kept being called Henrietta. Grandma's cataracts had become so invasive that it's a wonder she could see her neighbor's barn, let alone identify a single chicken.

She told me these stories when she was ninety-nine, shortly before her passing. Grandma had zero tolerance for idiots, hippies, and "that tricky Dick [Nixon]." She lived near Buck Creek in the sleepy non-descript town of Colburn, Indiana—an old coal stop for trains.

When I entered her house a rerun flickered on a waning brown and white tube with rolling horizontal lines. Just above the TV on the dated paneling sagged a drug store tapestry—a rug with painted deer. It was flanked by a dusty velvet painting of Jesus and a faded J.F.K., cockeyed in its frame. Sixty great-grandchildren formed a linear collage on a once-temporary shelf, and a plastic Sinclair dinosaur added a dot of faded green.

Seventy years earlier she began battling the world as a widow. Her immigrant husband had buckled under the weight of the Depression and resorted to self-immolation. Covered with white gas, he exited his world, but unfortunately, not hers. His charred body scarred her for life. Her hopes, love, and pleasant memories went up in smoke that day. Sad. Unfair. Unjustified. Where was God? Putting her determined face into the wind, she navigated the ensuing decades trusting only in herself. Or, so we surmised.

I crouched before her and talked loud and long. Grandma's glazed eyes began to gaze mysteriously deep into my soul. So...I revealed it. I begged, "Grandma, please hear me. I love you. I want to see you in heaven. Please, get your spiritual house in order." I caught myself yelling into her foggy eyes. I begged her to "Hear me!" I could feel her broad, proud shoulders through several layers of mixed patterns. My Grandma had lived a hard life. She thought she had conquered it, but in reality, it was about to conquer her. I thought I could see what she never could. I'll never forget her face that afternoon. Every deep crevasse told her story. Her eyes drooped half way down her cheeks. I held her loose, rough face in my hands for what I thought would be the last time. Geriatric Stoicism personified.

Even stubborn old Germans die and this one had just evaded the issue. Or had she? Had she heard me? I draped her snagged afghan across her knees and then rather lifelessly forced myself to the door.

Then she spoke.

"Jerry Allen, time to go." Just as unexpectedly, she rubbed those swollen spent sandpaper hands together, and started towards me. Her enlarged ankles had long since dwarfed her laced heeled boots, but she still wore them and managed a stiff shuffle. "I know, Grandma, I know. I just wanted to…" "Well get my coat, Jerry Allen, and let's go!" Suddenly, I wasn't leaving alone.

"To the cemetery, Jerry Allen. The cemetery." Her injunctions remained stern but were noticeably softer.

"I did it, Jerry Allen. I did it." Still proud, but with a purpose. "They said I couldn't do it but I did, Jerry Allen, I did it." She paused, put her gnarled hand on mine, and added, "All paid for. In cash, Jerry Allen. All taken care of." She ordered me to open her door then proclaimed, "I have something I want to show you, Jerry Allen."

I took her to the far southeast corner of the little Colburn cemetery where a tombstone edged its way up through the leaves. Several times I kicked the bunched leaves from in front of her methodical shuffle as we approached it. Though still unsure of what we were doing, the moment was obviously profound.

She slipped her arm out of mine and in slow motion sank her knees in the sod. With a few calculated passes she cleared the oak leaves from the face of her tombstone. Her guided, unsteady fingers followed her chiseled name. Then she outlined a cross and praying hands on the lower right corner. As she tilted her head to catch my eyes a weighty tear trickled at an angle down that old German face and disappeared into a crease. She kept tapping the cross, and assured me in her loud, raspy whisper, "I hear you, Jerry Allen. I hear you."

The trip back to her whitewashed little home was silent, one of resolve. As we made the last turn, a smile graced my face as I noticed the chicken farm. Grandma squeezed my hand.

As she stood at the end of her leafy walk, her half-wave proved to be final. She went to her eternal reward soon thereafter. She had made plans in silence. A beloved recluse had been listening for decades. Not to me, but to the steady understanding voice of her Creator.

Buck Creek Wisdom #27

"If eyes are windows to our souls, then don't mistake cataracts for blinds."

"Funerals have a way of etching our character in stone, and words are optional."

"Some people never stare death in the face, they just glance at it for decades."

Buck Creek & the Bible

"No, in all these things we are more than conquerors through him who loved us. For I am convinced that neither death nor life, neither angels nor demons, neither the present nor the future, nor any powers, neither height nor depth, nor anything else in all creation, will be able to separate us from the love of God that is in Christ Jesus our Lord." (Romans 8:37-39)

CHAPTER TWENTY-EIGHT:
Bad Hair Day: When Your Wig Falls Off in Junior High

You know it's a bad hair day when the basketball takes a funny bounce from the rim and knocks off your girlfriend's wig. You could hear a giant screeching sound on our sixth-grade playground—the earth stopping on its axis!

She had fooled me until that memorable hair removal. Her normal hair was awesome, so I didn't notice the difference. The only wigs I had seen were my grandmother's, and I swear she wore them backwards half the time. Seeing an otherwise gorgeous blonde in matted down, Bobby-pinned hair confused me. And, of course, my rolling on asphalt laughing uncontrollably immediately ended our pseudo-romance.

Why put something fake over something that is already beautiful?

A similar question was asked of former Miss California (2009) about her implants. After exuding a magnetic confidence in her stand against gay marriages, Carrie Prejean revealed her lack of confidence in her looks—ironically, after she had already won! Her augmentations caused people to question her moral authenticity.

When we try to make an impression, that's the impression we make.

123

We fall in love with a Paul Potts or Susan Boyle because the extraordinary comes from the ordinary. My hope is that besides assistance with dental problems and clothing, not much else changes with their looks. America has the same fascination with Crystal Bowersox and some of the "American Idol" contestants. And, we all hope that fame doesn't derail their inner beauty and sensibilities and land them in a Neverland Ranch. For some folks like Mitch Daniels and Jimmy Carter, wealth doesn't seem to faze them as they stay in touch with the common needs of both the rich and poor and can help and engage both. And that's extraordinary.

History is filled with human efforts to be something beyond what God provided. Whether it's Priscilla Presley's eerie plastic smile that debuted on *Dancing with the Stars*, Joan Rivers' self-effacing expressionless face, or Heidi Montag's ten plastic surgeries in a day, we don't have to flip the calendar very far back to find such examples.

In 1975, a few years after my girlfriend's sixth-grade synthetic head ordeal, Janis Ian's "At Seventeen" resonated with over a million LP buyers—and the host album won a Grammy. The lyrics are indeed riveting from the intense first line to the last:

> *I learned the truth at seventeen*
> *That love was meant for beauty queens*
> *And high school girls with clear skinned smiles*
> *Who married young and then retired.*
> *The valentines I never knew*
> *The Friday night charades of youth*
> *Were spent on one more beautiful*
> *At seventeen I learned the truth.*
> *And those of us with ravaged faces*
> *Lacking in the social graces*
> *Desperately remained at home*
> *Inventing lovers on the phone*
> *Who called to say come dance with me*
> *and murmured vague obscenities*
> *It isn't all it seems . . .at seventeen.*

The real kicker: she was an attractive teen! When I saw her album cover, I wish she had posted her phone number; and it wasn't to call the game warden to catch an ugly duckling. And her truthfully candid music was magnetic (see her "Society's Child," performed at 15-years-old on Smothers' Brothers—YouTube).

Her pain was real, but her self-worth unnecessarily devalued. Her autobiography (*Society's Child*, 2008) tells the rest of the story and background to her twenty-year marriage to another woman. Although I disagree with some of her choices, I appreciate her intense Alanis Morissette-ish reflection, both of self and society.

Perhaps it's a constant battle with parents to turn our kids' eyes from name brands to affordable quality, from peer pressure to priorities, and from ephemeral goals to lasting investments. I've had my day with platform shoes and plastic smiles, so to speak—we called them Cragar wheels, silk paisley shirts and IZODs.

The reality is God made each of us special, and regardless of purchased accessories, we're okay. Implants perhaps have their place, especially after lifesaving surgeries, but not in a beauty queen winner. However, I'm not a woman struggling with "ugly duckling" images, a cast member in *Miss Congeniality*, or dealing with overbearing parents living dreams through me.

Yeah, I'd like a different nose—a straight one. I suppose that would be all right since it'd be returning it to the way God made it. I'd like to be taller, and there are ways surgically to enhance my legs. I wish I could have been stronger during my weightlifting days, but I always passed on steroids. And I'd love to be a looker like Denzel Washington or Hugh Grant, but that ain't happenin' without a head transplant. The good part about being an author is that looks are optional, as well as height, strength and even style.

And speaking of style, writing about my weaknesses and impoverished beginnings in Buck Creek, Indiana launched a loyal following of readers. Books began to flow, broadcasts came my way, and "author" became more of a vocation than a dream.

It's funny, laughing and enjoying what once embarrassed me now engages readers. I wish the California beauty folks had realized that people would have embraced Carrie Prejean just the way she was—after all, they had already voted her queen.

BUCK CREEK: *True Stories to Tickle Your Mind*

Buck Creek Wisdom #28

"A special face is when the ordinary has the
countenance of the extraordinary."

"A special place is where the natural has been
touched by the supernatural."

"Most efforts to alter our faces aren't attempts to be God but are
surgical disagreements with his creative goodness."

"Beauty queens represent a democratic royalty
with no long term loyalty."

Buck Creek & the Bible

Whether we use the word "creation" or "nature," most of us would agree that a beauty exists totally apart from anything humans have created, and oftentimes, in spite of our irresponsible actions. The Bible is replete with references about focusing on God and his creation, including us, and not things of our own doing. "Can any one of you by worrying add a single hour to your life? 'And why do you worry about clothes? See how the flowers of the field grow. They do not labor or spin. Yet I tell you that not even Solomon in all his splendor was dressed like one of these.'" (Matthew 6:27-29)

Dr. Jerry Pattengale

CHAPTER TWENTY-NINE:
Driving in Circles

Plowing under pigs wasn't my plan. Huge scared sows squealed as this terrified twelve-year-old bounced alone in the tractor seat. When you're on a borrowed Allis Chalmers running down a farmer's income, it's not a pretty picture.

Mud flew. Tempers grew.

I pushed the brake pedal only to realize it locked and sent me in circles among hundreds of hogs just north of Idaville, Indiana. It was more like Amityville.

In a muddy barnyard on a heavy workday, laughter quickly dissipated. Expensive sows were in peril and the lone giant boar stood stunned and distraught. The tractor kept turning while his harem was squirming.

Random rampant squealing frightened me. Although I was from Buck Creek and familiar with some tractors, nothing prepared me for pig pandemonium. The farmer friend came running. While my cousin climbed the gate and laughed, others raised their hands and cursed. Cigarettes dropped and pigs flopped and my head spun. When I bumped the round metal pig feeder, a sense of urgency supplanted cautious optimism.

127

Woody Allen captions beneath those pigs would have read—"Can someone just tell the kid to turn off the key?"

"Look out!" came just as I baha'd a trough.

A sweaty, smoking farmhand finally mounted the possessed tractor, unlocked the pedal and restored order. A simple move saved a few sows.

Have you ever found yourself going in circles? Did your stomach drop as you noticed the same signposts over and over? Years later I would come across a historic episode in my studies that would shed light on spinning one's wheels.

After Buck Creek, I was fortunate to study history at Indiana Wesleyan University and at Jerusalem University College in Israel. Later, after a sidestep to a masters degree at Wheaton (IL), my terminal degrees were in ancient history at Miami University in Ohio. During that time, I came to understand more fully the dynamics of the legendary Hebrew leader, Samson—a major figure in the Judeo-Christian story.

Regardless of whether you believe in the supernatural aspect of the biblical narrative, it also contains a well-documented historical background that sheds incredible light on our ancestors.

The story of Samson, the Hebrew judge (or "president"), has been told in many forms today, and a luggage line carries his name and represents strength—Samsonite. The retelling of his story often highlights a sensuous woman, Delilah, who tricked him (Judges 13-16). In the biblical account, he receives supernatural strength then loses it by breaking his vow—his fault, regardless of the temptation. His enemies captured him, gauged out his eyes, and then put him in a grain mill. Eventually, the account notes that he regained his strength and was taken to Gaza; there he pushed a temple's central pillars apart and the building's collapse killed three thousand of his captors, the Philistines.

Well, for starters, archaeologists have found a Philistine temple from Samson's era that was indeed built on an architectural plan resting on two huge central pillars (at Qasile, a site in Tel Aviv—not the site of the story but corroborating evidence). Also, many of the ancient cities mentioned in Samson's accounts have been found, along with the types of historic gates that he allegedly removed and carried miles away. But for the sake of our discussion about going in circles, let's look at his time in the grain mill—his prison work.

Archeologists have found many mills from this era in which an ox or several men would push a lever in circles, thus grinding grain hour after hour, day after day. They were indeed going in circles. It's at this point that Samson began to realize that he had squandered his talents, and that he was getting nowhere toward his life calling (believing God had created and called him to fight the Philistines). He finally looked heavenward and had a serious discussion with God, and asked to get back on track: "Oh Sovereign Lord, remember me, just this once . . ." And, he eventually collapses the enemy's temple.

Many years ago, I used this biblical story to challenge a group of Olympic-bound athletes before the noted Fresno track relays in California. One of the runners had formerly run the anchor to defeat the gold-medal 400-relay team from the previous year (at UCLA's Olympic Stadium). However, he had suddenly changed, and though poor, was driving a BMW. With the Samson story in mind from my team devotional the previous evening, I walked to his table and jotted on a placemat the following poem for him: *I'm on the track, Round and round, An inner peace I have found. For the strength, To run free, O Sovereign Lord, Remember me.*

A week later, the track coach removed him from the team due to informed suspicions of drugs.

A couple of weeks later, he was caught smuggling drugs from an African country (swallowing balloons of heroin then passing them once returning to America). Only a few months earlier the leader of that country (his native home) would have had him executed—but a leadership and policy change landed him in a dungeon instead. Due to his celebrity status, he was released within the year but had been in the bowels of a remote penal system, nearly forgotten for life.

About a year after the incident, he came walking across the track in his civilian clothes, greeting me before a college meet started. He was on suspension from competition, but would one day run again. He smiled, then reached into his wallet and pulled out the poem torn from the corner of the worn placemat—"I'm on the track, round and round . . ."

The next time you find yourself plowing in circles, pushing the same lever round and round, or deeply alone and in unwanted isolation, find your focus. For those who believe in the supernatural—it's upward then inward. For others, there needs to be some focus outside yourself for inner reflection.

And by the way, no pigs were injured in the writing of this story, only a barnyard and a boy's pride.

Buck Creek Wisdom #29

"If you feel far from God, guess who moved."

"To put your best foot forward, you need to take the first step."

"For those who believe in the supernatural—it's upward then inward to find focus. For those who only believe in the natural, you're on your inward own."

Buck Creek & the Bible

Trust in the Lord with all your heart and lean not on your own understanding; in all your ways submit to him, and he will make your paths straight." (Proverbs 3:5-6)

CHAPTER THIRTY:
Buck Creek Golf

He asked for advice on his club selection. I replied, "The one you feel most comfortable with." It was my first time caddying. I had never golfed.

The pot-bellied businessman pulled out a two iron, threw down his thin cigar, adjusted his polyester button-down, and swung away.

It was the shot of his life—powerfully sailing with a slight draw. It one-hopped to the front of the green, rolled slightly left and nestled near the pen.

"Kid, you're a genius!"

My advice worked only once. For sixteen more holes I lugged his overstuffed ostrich skin bag and kept quiet. I spent a year on the course that day—for $4.00 and a used golf ball.

Until then, I had never entered the course gate—a stone boundary to nonmembers. It represented access to a country club, and we were country boys without clubs. Members drank fine wine. Our parents drank Falls City beer. Members drove shiny sedans and some smoked Tiparillos. We passed by in jerry-rigged trucks with gun racks and toolboxes while our dads smoked filterless Camels. Members worked wonders with Ping and Titleist; we worked with Craftsman and salvaged titles.

Financially and culturally, access to golf was unthinkable and undesirable.

I had been on that course one other time, but long after sunset and over a side fence. The seniors took us "rookies" snipe hunting. The initiation passed quietly, except for one overzealous Buck Creek boy.

He yelled "Snipe! Snipe!" and took off with his gunnysack. Hoopin' and hollerin,' he jumped toward it—only to become stunned by a skunk's foul spray. Whatever a snipe is, it is not white striped with a black tail. The upperclassmen abandoned the sorry-smellin' misguided sniper. He had no luck hitchhiking either. After a few days of tomato juice baths, he finally returned to the jeers of the school hallway.

While caddying, I was more interested in seeing the skunk episode site in the daylight than replacing chunks of grass from my golfer's low swings. For some reason, the guy kept tearing up the expensive grass.

Golf courses were also funny, foreign places to my dad and uncles. Other than Cubs and Purdue games on garage radios, sports were not part of their tough lives and time-clocked weeks.

Access to college seemed just as inaccessible and foreign.

Although Purdue was nearby, passing through campus might as well have been Oz—it was a strange land. Besides a field trip to watch Bob Ford and Rick Mount practice basketball and a Christmas banquet, the college campus was someone else's world. I remember sitting in the front row in Mackey arena in awe of a building that could house our town. The floor was eye level, and the basketball players were giants. They were TV people. But little did I know that teachers were trying to show me the yellow brick road. Like Upward Bound college programs for first-generation students, they knew that part of the barrier to college was becoming familiar with the experience.

A concerned school counselor, scholarships and Pell grant aid helped open the door. Through "Dr. Brewer's" history lectures and a relentless recruiter—a self-imposed guardian of my college future—at sixteen, I was on my way to Indiana Wesleyan University with all bills paid.

Access is more than money; it's also a mindset. The applicant needs a desire and a plan, and the institutions need to plan for such desires.

New knowledge begged new answers. Dr. Brewer had an uncanny way of taking a simple unprovoked mind and turning it on. Suddenly, my world became a bit larger than grease guns and hunting seasons. For the first time, I wanted to learn beyond my situation. The lights went on, and I was home. Yes, I began to dream. I began to listen to this one-time college gibberish. Access started to mean opportunity. The opaque admission door started to become transparent.

Like admission to the golf club, access included a mindset—both for the potential member and the institution. College personnel pulled while those at high school pushed. And somewhere in the process, I began to grab hold.

Forty years later, access has a new challenge—the financial aid door remains opaque. Students are beginning to dream but find it increasingly difficult to go through the door—no matter who is pushing and pulling.

For many apartment-laden communities, financial assistance isn't keeping pace with the tuition costs—they can't afford the membership fees. The Pell grant has about one-fourth the buying power for today's Buck Creek kids than in 1975. Likewise, their parents cannot afford special SAT study courses or academic prep camps. And, in turn, their children will likely miss the best scholarships. Many of these kids are rather gifted students, and they may gain access later in life—but after missing a decade of opportunities.

Access to college has led to fulfillment and fun in a rather complex and chaotic time. Most importantly, it's allowed me to understand my life calling, yes, a purpose-guided life.

There will always be exclusive clubs and colleges, but the mindset I'm thrilled about is one that sees concerned golfers and academics striving to ensure access to the playing field at some level. My home course is not Pebble Beach, but it's my connection to such an experience and for some gifted members to believe that Tiger's, Rory's and Phil's world is within reach. Our college is not Harvard, but our students engage in the same life-changing dialogue, in the same "great debate," but with a clearer mission. Some would rate Indiana Wesleyan, Taylor, Huntington, Bethel, Anderson and similar universities at the top of the list for this very reason.

A few years ago, I took an African American nine-year-old for his first golfing experience. He lost eight of my balls in the second-hole pond. But like that pot-bellied businessman forty years ago, he'll long remember that shot that sailed to the green (even if it was his twenty-sixth stroke). It was his experience, his struggle and eventual joy from inside the gate. The next week, I took my seventy-two-year-old friend, Johnny Taylor, for his first round. He noted that as an African American, he simply hadn't been invited earlier in life. And yes, we sure laughed out loud at the second-hole pond. It proved to be his only outing before his passing a few months later.

The PGA has successfully launched programs to open its gates to the Buck Creek types and to the young Johnny Taylors. And many groups are trying to do the same for colleges.

The "Dr." title before my name dangles as a membership card to the academy, and the "Arbor Trace" card on my bag identifies membership in a club. I'm not good enough to get mad at a bad shot but hopeful that people at least get one. As for the young boy (Michael) who hit those balls into the pond—he's now about 6'9" and this spring won a national high jumping contest. He's also in college with full tuition covered. He'll jump higher in life through this educational access.

And for those still finding your way—just don't hit a skunk with a stick, because the smell will follow you for life.

Buck Creek Wisdom #30

"Access is more than money, it's also a mindset."

"A disenfranchised applicant needs a desire and plan, and institutions need to plan for such desires."

"Remember that at some point raising the bar eliminates everyone, and that some successes are measured by the level you've failed."

Buck Creek & the Bible

A clear biblical theme is the role of humility regardless of our rank in life, and oftentimes its presence is inextricably linked to our sustained success. "Humble yourselves, therefore, under God's mighty hand, that he may lift you up in due time." (1 Peter 5:6) "He holds success in store for the upright, he is a shield to those whose walk is blameless." (Proverbs 2:7)

Dr. Jerry Pattengale

CHAPTER THIRTY-ONE:
The Poster Girls of Buck Creek: Natural Beauty and Mature Eyes

Ginger of *Gilligan's Island* had a smooth baritone voice and facial mole that captured our collective soul. She was our Buck Creek hottie. Why the Professor kept trying to leave the island was beyond us! And so began our string of Buck Creek poster girls.

In junior high, it was Barbara Eden in her Jeannie jammies. Ellie May Clampett's "Gee-whiz" simplicity made us googly-eyed. Wonder Woman hypnotized us with her two-fisted hip pose and frontal armor. Farah Fawcett's red swimsuit poster decorated our late 1970s dorm rooms. And after *Grease*, we'd go into our Travolta swagger, comb one side of our hair, and sing "You're the one that I want!" while holding Olivia's Newton John's LP cover. Of course, this occurred against a spontaneous backdrop of musically challenged guys humming the chorus— "Ooh, ooh, ooh!"

I suppose most boys have been fascinated with beautiful women, and the same is true of men-boys. My grandpa had Rockwell's *Rosie the Riveter* picture next to a Hudson hubcap above his workbench, and his sons had a Marilyn Monroe shrine in their uptown garage. Many centuries earlier, the Italians had their Mona Lisa fascinations, the English Tudors their Anne Boleyn, the Romans their first-century

137

wall paintings at Pompeii, the Egyptians their Nefertiti reliefs and the Babylonians their clay busts of Inanna.

Cindy (my wife) and I shouldn't have been surprised when our "adopted", teenage, Chinese "sons" gave us a wooden inlay of Ancient China's "Four Great Beauties." Their legendary looks allegedly caused the moon to shy away, fish to become so entranced that they forgot to swim and sank, and birds to forget to fly and plummeted to earth.

God created us to recognize beauty, and though culturally influenced in some aspects, all non-reprobate humans continue to be stunned by the spectacular. Princess Di's face appearing on a storefront's large screen can stop traffic. Likewise, a double rainbow can prompt Chicago employees nearly to tip the Sears Tower by all running to office windows. And like C. S. Lewis, we lock onto natural landscape standards such as Shadowlands that forever frame our thoughts of tranquil beauty.

Artists captivate us with creative representations of beauty, such as Chihuly's blown glass series, "Seaforms." When I recently turned the first corner in the Columbia, South Carolina museum, one of his masterpieces literally took my breath away. The six-foot, bright yellow, transparent, fanned glass magnified natural beauty; it arrested my unsuspecting mind. Another Chihuly in a Salt Lake City museum mesmerized me when I realized that the bright 20-foot tower is actually hundreds of his interwoven creations. The one in the Oklahoma City Museum of Art is even larger and fascinated me on several visits.

I had a similar experience in Indiana Wesleyan University's art gallery a few years ago upon seeing Rod Crossman's "Fantasy" series. While the central painting was still leaning against the wall awaiting mounting, the light caught its painted Venus statue. She dazzled. I froze. She was standing there on canvas, in an unexpected place—a virgin pond deep within a thick forest. Painted just beyond was a surprised angler making the discovery as he walked through the last clump of trees. With fly rod still in hand, he too had that frozen look of fascination. The famous master artist had somehow captured the essence of unexpected beauty.

Crossman's paintings again stunned me while selecting a piece for Father Hesburgh (former president of Notre Dame, who loves fly fishing).

It had been nearly thirty years since I had been in the hallowed upper halls of the Crossman chalet just south of Marion, Indiana. His invitation was a treat: ". . . to come upstairs and look at a few canvases." I vividly recalled my last trip up those same stairs decades earlier. Every piece invited me in, all tugging at my dormant memories of childhood fishing—of those secret serene places.

Before turning left into a cryptic repository, almost like entering a Jewish genizah, I stopped on the stairs to absorb a painted scene arresting my thoughts. Then another, and finally, I asked Rod to select a painting for Father Hesburgh. I don't think that beauty is in the eyes of the beholder but beheld by the eyes. In time, the mind helps the eyes to understand more fully, to become "trained eyes"— they'll always be our windows into God's kaleidoscopic mysteries of life. And we're also reminded in this fallen world, accented by 9/11's ills, that when people fail to see and respect such beauty they tend to espouse barbaric values.

I enjoy beautiful things more deeply than imaginable in my Buck Creek youth, more profoundly than at face value of our poster girls. Even more than the master paintings are pictures I've enjoyed for over twenty years.

Sometimes it's a glimpse of Cindy's especially magnetic face I catch from across a crowded room. Or it's her deep smile visible through the kitchen window while she chats on her cell phone. Or her flushed face and glimmering eyes while receiving too much attention. My wife's beauty isn't just skin deep, it's also deep within her skin. It's in her soul and manifest in all that surfaces. It's a masterpiece whether in person or painted by a master.

Beauty is not to be taken for granted, but granted for the taking—maturity is what we do with it and for it. From people to pets to the planet, there are beautiful things that demand our best thinking.

And, I suppose today there are a few Hannah Montana posters hanging in some Buck Creek tree houses, but there's hope that their owners will learn to appreciate a deeper beauty and decades from now at a class reunion laugh while they hum "The Best of Both Worlds."

Buck Creek Wisdom #31

"Beautiful things demand our best thinking and underpin our best theology."

"Beauty is not in the eyes of the beholder but beheld by the eyes."

"The richest beauty isn't just skin deep, it's also deep within one's skin."

"Beauty is not to be taken for granted, but granted for the taking — maturity is what we do with it and for it."

Buck Creek & the Bible

The Bible has various passages that highlight pure beauty that is in alignment with God's intended purpose, such as Jesus's word recorded in Matthew 6:28-29: "And why do you worry about clothes? See how the lilies of the field grow. They do not labor or spin. Yet I tell you that not even Solomon in all his splendor was dressed like one of these." The Bible is also rather candid about "beautiful" things being out of alignment: "Like a gold ring in a pig's snout is a beautiful woman who shows no discretion." (Proverbs 11:22) Ezekiel recognizes the splendor of the seemingly impregnable city of Tyre, while prophesizing its doom because its king thought he was "as wise as a god." He writes "what the Sovereign Lord says," "I am going to bring foreigners against you, the most ruthless of nations; they will draw their swords against your beauty and wisdom and pierce your shining splendor." (Ezekiel 28: 7)

Dr. Jerry Pattengale

CHAPTER THIRTY-TWO:
Losing Your Marbles

While looking out the window of our English castle, I chuckled, "I'm a long way from Buck Creek, Indiana."

Smart business deals had afforded our patron the opportunity to buy this 185-room wonder near the Welsh border and to send me there to write its history.

He learned the rules of the business game, the nature of its players, and managed to win millions more than he lost. From complex bids at Sotheby's, visceral calls on stocks, and deft Wall Street maneuvers, he won. He occasionally reminisced about business lessons he had learned as a student, and I think we can all relate.

My first business lessons occurred during recesses outside the bulky brick school in Buck Creek. We called the course "Marbles."

We'd brag about our new cat-eyes and shooters (the larger ones). Lines were drawn in the matted dust, and the rules were simple. All understood.

If Johnny knocked your marble across the line, you forfeited it. Or, if you lost the most marbles, Johnny could have his pick—even your new silver.

To lose one's marbles was the ultimate disaster. Kids pointed. Jokes flew. Lunchtime swaps of *Hostess* fruit pies for mediocre marbles ensued.

At day's end, the contents in that leather pouch, bouncing against your Levis, was another lesson learned—profit or loss. The long walk down the aisle of that snub-nosed bus became a victory march, or a gauntlet of victors.

You either snatched the prize or served as prize money. Either way, you chose to play and knew the rules.

And, generally, the "Johnnys" were well established. When these perennial champs lined up to pitch their marbles against the limestone footer to determine matches, the drawstring on your pouch remained tight. The risk seemed too high: the competition too keen.

Decades later, business principles once again dominate the landscape. The likes of Enron and Bernie Madoff took all the marbles from hosts of peoples. They erased the lines and dipped into pouches without us knowing the strings had been opened. Athletes are also not exempt. Barry Bonds' repeated attempts to reestablish the veneer of credibility of his juiced-homerun swings. The meteoric fall of Lance Armstrong. Many leadingbankers have also been deemed incredulous, including the $108 million settlement for homeowners fleeced by Countrywide Home Loans, Inc.—tactics that included inflated and false charges and even $300 lawn cuts. And what about the fast moving coach, Pete Carroll? He seems to have sprinted away cleanly from the Reggie-Bush violations, and innocent student athletes were punished. And the epitome of avarice surrounds the Penn State debacle and the late Joe Paterno's sad demise.

In 2001, I coined the term "enronic" in my newsprint column a week before comedian Dennis Miller used it in a monologue. *Enronic* refers to anyone who erases the line and takes marbles from the unsuspecting and/or powerless. In short, an *enronic* deal is unethical in a specific sense—business executives profiting from customers or lesser partners denied access to the business deal itself.

Unlike Buck Creek, the lines were erased and the peer review absent.

Our castle patron, the late Robert Van Kampen, warned me of such deals.

While chatting in his five-story home overlooking Lake Michigan, I asked about his business philosophy, his secrets to success.

"Jerry," he began while clutching his Disney mug in front of the Rembrandt near his elevator, "two things you should never forget: The right of a second decision, and treat business partners as if they're snakes."

He expounded before I could respond.

"Through the years I've made two, three, sometimes ten decisions before my competitors made one."

I managed to ask, "Your snake theory seems harsh. Would you treat friends the same?"

His free hand flung wildly and coffee drops flew as he stood, "You bet! The Bible informs us that we're all fallen individuals with a bent to sin."

As the months passed I began to understand, witnessing many potential partners slither into his office with hidden agendas. Money, especially piles of it, invites the disingenuous.

His advice could have saved this Buck Creek boy from an enronic encounter with an educational consulting firm. After some international success with a top-ten visited website, I turned my technological eyes (now lost to Future Shock cataracts) to aiding student success through a creative program—digital pictorial directories, advising tracking, etc.

Numerous conference and campus presentations followed, and by 1999, it garnered a national education award (NACADA).

The consulting firm's president invited me to his corporate office, sent two of his VPs to our campus on two occasions and slated me at his company's national conference. His VPs signed nondisclosure agreements. The lines were drawn.

Then came the enronic moment. After eighteen months and repeated requests for a response from the firm, the Buck Creek boy met education's Enron.

While at a conference, my heart dropped when a digital page—identical to one my team created—appeared on screen. The firm had prostituted my program.

"The price for this program is $75,000," announced the same VP who months earlier bragged in my office about my program's appeal elsewhere. Then he added, "And a slimmer version is available for only $30,000!"

The cost of a David-Goliath legal battle was beyond my means. I ran into a snake, dear patron, an enronic python.

Enronic deals disrupt timing, and in the technology market, timing is virtually everything.

Enronic deals dislodge resources and disguise reputations, but true character stands the test of time.

In my little Indiana schoolyard, an attempt to erase lines or miscount marbles was about the only thing worse than losing. Like Hester Prynne, the cheater's "C" went with you.

Reputations may not buy your marbles, but they'll get invitations to more important games.

My Buck Creek school is gone, but not the lessons of lines and peer review. After nearly forty years, I reconnected with my childhood friend, Howard, as he enrolled his bright daughter in our college. Howard was one of those few kids who always recognized the value of lines and lining up with integrity. It's no surprise that he's raised a stellar young woman with strong character, and decades later there still exists a bond between us because of mutual and perpetual respect for similar lines.

As for business, there's the "right way" and the "other way," and both ways can cost you your marbles, but the latter also chips away at your name.

Buck Creek residents eventually replaced our marble haven with a picturesque Little League diamond.

Enjoy the fences, kids. Some day, when the stakes are higher, people you trust may pull the posts while your homerun ball is still in flight.

Buck Creek Wisdom #32

"Reputations may not buy your marbles, but they'll get invitations to more important games."

"Enronic deals pay ephemeral dividends."

"Business has the right way and the other way, and both may lose your marbles but only one your reputation."

Buck Creek & the Bible

The Bible is replete with candid comments about the ills of avarice. "The greedy bring ruin to their households, but the one who hates bribes will live." (Proverbs 15:27) "The greedy stir up conflict, but those who trust in the Lord will prosper." (Proverbs 28:25) "Watch out! Be on your guard against all kinds of greed; life does not consist in an abundance of possessions." (Luke 12:15)

CHAPTER THIRTY-THREE:
Shooting Grandma on July Fourth

When my bottle rockets began pummeling my grandmother, our July Fourth party exploded.

I had stacked them on an old water heater near the hog roast. How was I to know that my Dad's cigarette would roll in the wind?

Slightly wedged between the short pipes atop the heater, one random spark became a sinister wick. With Gatlin gun repetition, the horizontal missiles developed GPS—Granny Positioning System.

Grandma Pattengale was caught in the crosshairs.

The first explosion scared everyone, not the least our maturely-dressed matriarch.

Nailed her.

Swwooooshh—Pow!! Nailed her again.

Her quasi-Jitterbug during the rapid fire was of no avail.

Pow! Pow—pow—pow—pow! And then, Ow! Ow—ow—ow—ow!

Those geriatric Tomahawk rockets would have found her anywhere, even behind the nearby monster truck.

Rockets that missed still seemed to position for the next hit.

Corporate laughter turned to panic. The only peaceful face was the basking hog's smile on the rotisserie.

With a mix of Sugar Ray moves saddled with George Forman speed, she ducked and bobbed, and weaved side to side—but always a bit too late.

Whap, whap—Bang! Bang! Yep, nailed her again, and again, and then, POW!!, again . . .

Her last jaunt was almost miraculous—she Tim-Conway-shuffled far from the smoking heater, yep, for one final direct hit! The rocket did an elliptical turn and followed, and, yep—Shhhhhhhhh—BAM!

Amid the charcoaled rockets, pork pit, bon fire, chain smokers, silent banjoes and half-empty long-neck bottles, a hazy pandemonium ensued. While Grandma was getting blasted an eight-track blasted The Buckaroos music. "My Heart Skips a Beat" never sounded the same.

Like secret service agents a day late to Ford's Theater, one uncle finally shielded her while another doused the few remaining rockets with Falls City.

Except for a burn mark on her hose, Grandma escaped unharmed. She would either light up my bottom or smack the smile off the spinning pig and set a rotisserie RPM record. The latter was safe.

When order restored, an uncle began smacking his pack of Camels while saying, "D*$%*! That was more exciting than the Columbia Park!"

It was a July Fourth tradition for many of the Buck Creek families to attend fireworks at the Lafayette park.

Fourth of July was celebrated religiously, the park one night and family outings the next.

Nearly all of the male adults around that hog roast had served in the military, and the Fourth resonated with a sense of personal accomplishment. Although few had finished high school, they had experiential learning of utmost importance.

My Grandpa Saubert, neighbor of my Pattengale grandparents on one side and Great-Grandparent Pattengales on the other (where Uncle Buck would later inhabit), had nearly lost his leg in WWII. While helping to liberate Europeans, a land mine ended his tour of duty and prompted his premature return to Buck Creek where a faded picture of him atop a toppled Nazi wall remains.

My relatives have served from Korea, Vietnam and Kuwait to Ft. Bragg and Monticello. VFWs and AmVets are more than unknown letters on faded marques. American flags remain sacred—especially those diamond folds from veteran funerals.

These men reverenced democracy and cherished freedom.

Their simple pre-war, no-collar lives were remote and independent. Hunting and mushrooming. Scrapping old cars. Piling cords of wood and unseemly old pallets. Building high-octane go carts. Hosting impromptu rat shoots in corn sheds. Chopping '57 Chevys for dirt track races. Roasting pigs with first names. Playing Jack Daniels Euchre until the cows came home—literally.

They were free, and had fought to protect it during their only extended times outside of Indiana back country. They saw firsthand the contrast to freedom—totalitarianism and communism, humanity's ills unchecked.

My uncles had witnessed abstract thoughts intersecting concrete results—cement human furnaces, pill boxes and razed orphanages.

They had learned that great minds could produce the greatest of errors, that education without humanitarian values often enhanced horrid inhumane goals.

Undoing oppressive governments strengthened their love for American judicial foundations.

Stench from decentralized sewer systems was several flights away from rock bass fishing on Sugar Creek.

Hollow, holocaust survivor eyes staring at newfound freedom opened their own eyes to Constitutional protection and rights.

Scraggly, infected cats scampering from open garbage piles reaffirmed Americans' establishment of humane shelters and abatement plans.

Abandoned, fly-covered children accented their appreciation for child protection laws and the United Way.

Ravaged, lifeless churches reminded them of democratic foundations that protected core beliefs and institutions of hope—and also their right to avoid attendance.

Assassinations and attempted coups brought respect for American political parties that could rally for common goals.

For my relatives, the Fourth is a time to celebrate contrasts. Regardless of life choices and personal successes and failures, it's a time of common pride.

At many Buck Creek funerals, the playing of taps evokes memories of the proudest episode of their hard lives—their fight for a people's freedom and the protection of democratic ideals. Their link to the Valley Forges and Pat Tillmans. And "Proud to Be an American" has become an annual teary-eyed favorite.

That hog roast in the late 1960s remains a snapshot of the Fourth in its fullness.

Grandma would outlive many that celebrated that Fourth fiasco. But she also lived to see some of her sixty grandchildren finish college, many endorse religion, some interracially marry, a few become Democrats, and some choose military careers. All remained free, and one has resided in her house since her passing.

She also lived to see bottle rocket laws develop and civility issues take center stage.

In the end, Grandma died of natural causes in a remarkable country where it seems natural to do so.

Buck Creek Wisdom #33

"The greater the mind, the chance for the greater error."

"Cherishing freedom in the long-term requires reverencing democracy in the short-term."

"Both cathedrals and concentration camps are the manifestation of abstract thoughts intersecting concrete results."

"Our constitutional and ecclesiastic foundations share the same cornerstone."

Buck Creek & the Bible

Several songs in the Christian tradition highlight the "foundation" of Christ in our lives, such as "On Christ the solid rock I stand, all other ground is sinking sand . . ." Jesus uses this same metaphor, and expounds on it in his Sermon on the Mount: "Therefore everyone who hears these words of mine and puts them into practice is like a wise man who built his house on the rock. The rain came down, the streams rose, and the winds blew and beat against that house; yet it did not fall, because it had its foundation on the rock. But everyone who hears these words of mine and does not put them into practice is like a foolish man who built his house on sand. The rain came down, the streams rose, and the winds blew and beat against that house, and it fell with a great crash." (Matthew 7:24-27)

CHAPTER THIRTY-FOUR:
Bottoms Up in Buck Creek

My three pairs of underwear didn't blunt the principal's spanking.

"Okay Mr. Pattengale, bend over and hold the desk with both hands" was the precursor to the smack heard around the world—well, at least in our little non-descript town northeast of Lafayette.

He tricked me. After giving me a night to think about my infraction (and a chance to pad the target zone), he touched "The Board of Education" to my padded bottom. However, as I steadied my boney body for his legendary whack, and somewhat grinned knowing I had prepared for this with extra cushion, he whipped me on my hamstrings!

System failure! Shock! A Woody Allen caption would have read – "Aahhhhhhhhhhhh!"

Have you ever tried so hard not to cry you looked constipated? My defining moment was faking a normal walk and not waddling past the others about to get the same, lined up outside the opaque glass door. I had planned to say, "Sir, thank you for the encouragement!" Instead, my numb body had the rigidity of Al Gore at a karaoke bar. I had received plenty of willow branch whippings at home, but this felt like ten syringes of cortisone, or worse, like being trapped in the

Sears Tower elevator with Yoko Ono music playing through Bose speakers. Even the newsroom scene of Steve Carrel in *Bruce Almighty* wouldn't have helped me to fake smile.

The principal had some real rascals to contend with, farm boys with no filters, and his discipline seemed to work. I had heard of "The Board of Education" but didn't know it had quarter-inch holes drilled in it. My hamstrings looked like a Parcheesi board for a week. I didn't cry until I was alone in a bathroom stall, but stayed way too long to convince my buddies that it didn't hurt. They also sat rather gingerly in their seats. I was especially bummed when the girl in our group of misfits didn't get the same treatment, only a caution not to hang around riffraff—and she had the real personality of Cruella de Vil.

Our big crime? Laughing uncontrollably at our biology teacher for attempting to put a dying raccoon out of its misery (hit on the road in front of the school). As he stuffed it in a huge jar of formaldehyde, he obviously had forgotten Archimedes's Displacement Theory—liquid spewed from the jar, stinking the room and causing a school evacuation. We were elated, until the deep principal's voice came over the speakers calling a few of us by name back into the building. It would prove to be ephemeral popularity.

Our bottoms paid the price the next day, wishing for huge snow cones for seats.

Much more serious episodes occur in which all our preparation cannot entirely alleviate pain, or its anticipation. Ask our son.

We've been learning about the throes of his leukemia, though he's the only one that can endure treatments, pain, spinal tap routines, the unknown and the predictable.

One of his many regimens involves trips to Riley Hospital (now IU North) in Carmel, Indiana—where his great (and well-named) Dr. "Lazarus" monitors a successful protocol.

To ease patients' pain, the protocol for shots of the enzyme Asparagines is no longer stretched over a few days and nine injections, but one trip with a remarkable orchestration.

At thirty miles, our halfway point to Riley Hospital, Nick rubs numbing cream on the fronts of his quad muscles. After initial pleasantries at the hospital, four medical staff members (by now, his good friends) surround Nick with loaded syringes. Flat on his back, he clinches his jaw, knowing that on the count of three they'll all inject him simultaneously. And they do.

As his father, I sat there the first time amazed at the procedure, the professionalism, the caution, the timing. Each of the four attendants answered accountability and safety questions from the good doctor, then came something I really wasn't ready for: "One, two, three!" Stab, stab, stab, stab. Nick's body mildly jolted and seemed to levitate—enduring the simultaneous syringes.

I suddenly got clammy, nauseous, and leaned against the wall trying not to faint. And just as quickly it was over. Nick sat up, began chatting with his medical cadres and before long was joking about bad Nicholas Cage films.

My mind raced trying to catch up to my heart. I had just witnessed what few had, and a cryptic part of his journey that his throng of friends will likely never comprehend. I cried to God, both wanting to be of more help and also thankful that there is a positive prognosis—and the good doctors have helped alleviate pain through aggressive protocols. And, of course, helping to prevent the harshest of pains when one's child ceases to breathe. We're blessed and thankful for good news. In this case, calculated pain leads to healthy gains.

There's a pride that swells in a father's heart when he sees firsthand a son's brave spirit and an accompanying sadness when shocked with the reality of his struggle. Whether in Marion, Indiana, Kabul, or Rwanda, when a child grimaces our gut wrenches. And when a recovering child smiles, our heart brightens. Pain comes in many forms, and as we continue to make donations to medical research, colleges, Family Services and likeminded agencies, in part we're helping children with its reality.

Buck Creek Wisdom #34

"Calculated pain can lead to healthy gains though oftentimes emotion drives the algorithm."

"The best prognosis for cancer is preventing it from devouring hope."

"A child's disease reminds us that finiteness and fairness are defined but not determined by humans."

Buck Creek & the Bible

It's difficult to think of positives in the presence of adversity or setbacks, but trials are a part of life we need to handle, or they'll handle us. "Consider it pure joy, my brothers and sisters, whenever you face trials of many kinds, because you know that the testing of your faith produces perseverance. Let perseverance finish its work so that you may be mature and complete, not lacking anything." (James 1:2-4)

| Dr. Jerry Pattengale

CHAPTER THIRTY-FIVE:
I Didn't See a Corvair at the White House

My first car didn't go far. It was a recycled, dull-white Corvair.

My first "road trip" covered an eventful five miles and took about three hours and an extra three quarts of oil. My football buddy helped push it home. His big round forehead was wetter than the dew-covered bowling ball mounted in my uncle's lawn.

For a few minutes that day we were styling—the breeze blowing through our Bee-Gee-style hair as our nostalgic convertible rolled through town. Our teen vanity craved an audience.

But when we hit the railroad track in town center, the motor mount broke; oil started shooting out the dipstick and smoke bellowed. Our BP moment wasn't pretty. We rolled back through town again, hoping against the odds that nobody saw or smelled us. I felt like the Marty Feldman hunchback in *Young Frankenstein*. But instead of "What hump?" I was asking, "What smoke?"

I should have been concerned when we pulled the motor from a defunct junkyard. Weeds ensconcing the manifold. A random clutch plate leaning on the block caked in dirt. Yep, somehow my excitement to have a car—a convertible, no less—loomed larger than logic.

After weeks with experimental mechanics, we cruised again. This time it took about four quarts to get to town—and we eventually rolled back into our driveway behind a makeshift tow chain.

In time, I realized that we had it all wrong. Instead of using it as a car, the Corvair served better as a doghouse. Our Saint Bernard loved it. The car became a backyard fixture—an acceptable lawn ornament in my Buck Creek culture.

I then purchased an Oldsmobile 98—friends kept asking for a ride in the ark. Next came the other extreme—a Spider Fiat. A fun car, until the passenger seat began falling through its rusted floorboard and ill-conceived *uniframe*.

My Cutlass Supreme was a welcome change, but soon the new design of the now laughable Gremlin won me over. I traded for the wedge-on-wheels and lived with my choice for the next six years.

But that's the key: the souped-up, silly looking Ralph-Nader-slammed ratty ride with ill-designed doors and a leaky back hatch lasted through college and beyond. It was dependable until smashed by another Nader-tagged car, a Pinto.

In time, I drove a vintage Mercedes—which lasted for a decade. However, with four boys in private schools, for years I drove a '96 Taurus bequeathed by our great-aunt. At my age, dependability trumps style.

And that's the way I view institutions and their leaders—dependability over style. With age come experience and a reluctance to sacrifice substance for style. In election years, we tend to look at mayoral and presidential candidates like cars. Some keep running on salvage titles. Others might be showing their age, but what a nice ride they've provided. A few are considered classics—regardless of political parties, a resounding consensus recognizes their unique status. Young or old, we realize their unique giftedness and statesmanship. Perhaps President Reagan and Winston Churchill are among the best examples, and President Carter for living out a legacy of compassion.

We're living in a time when a statue of a man, the Rev. Billy Graham, lives out his life's apparent final decade with the same class as his previous eighty. If he were a Chevy, few would buy Fords, or vice versa. He stands behind a pulpit and beacons the same world that knocks often on his modest door of sustained integrity. His steady performance, brilliant glimmer in his eyes, and hallmark message silence millions. We look for politicians with either the legitimate promise of such dependability, or the legacy of such.

Classic cars have a unique character that stands the test of time. At fifty-four years old, that's what I want. I've got some dents to fix, but at least I'm aware they exist. I'm approaching a season in life that'll likely see my motor mount crack a few times before it finally breaks. I'll probably realize fluid level problems and see other warning lights. And I'll change several flat tires in addition to keeping my midriff spare. Yes, I'm already due for a new paint job.

Like Rev. Graham, when the paint begins to fade I hope solid metal shows through. He's shown us that consistent logic, high moral standards, and follow-through always trump silver-tongued oration, even for brilliant communicators. During election seasons the primary question should never be if Biden is boring, if Obama is hip or if Romney is refreshing. The strength of one's leadership is inextricably linked to one's performance.

A couple of years ago, I attended a meeting in the White House and gazed down its hallowed halls and framed reminders of dependability. While the decorations and architectural appointments grabbed my attention, the historical displays of courage and character sustain it. Some of our past presidents and state leaders have blown gaskets, acquired dents and sported odd paint jobs—but their character has stood the test of time.

I recently met with a man whose business sold for billions. Not once did we talk about what type of cars we drive, but what drives us. And that kept me smiling as I approached our Chrysler van with 188,000 miles—with indentations that give it character.

Buck Creek Wisdom #35

"Corvairs remind us that creativity is a job half done."

"Strong leaders are less preoccupied with what
we drive than with what drives us."

"It's never a good sign when an audience smells
you before they see you and it's even worse when they hear
you and then think you stink."

"With age comes experience, and with maturity a
reluctance to sacrifice substance for style; unfortunately
longevity does not ensure logic."

Buck Creek & the Bible

The Apostle Paul reminded the Church at Corinth (in Greece) of the need to mature in both thought and action and ultimately the eternal perspective. "When I was a child, I talked like a child, I thought like a child, I reasoned like a child. When I became a man, I put the ways of childhood behind me. For now we see only a reflection as in a mirror; then we shall see face to face. Now I know in part; then I shall know fully, even as I am fully known." (1 Corinthians 13:11-12) I lived in Corinth as part of an archeology research team with the National Endowment of the Humanities; I was reminded by both the artifacts and the ancient literature of various entertainment and pagan choices confronting Paul and the Corinthians. In this passage, he reminds them and us that we see but a reflection—but we do see enough to know the truth.

CHAPTER THIRTY-SIX:
Waking Up with the Answers

Some practical jokes make us laugh for decades. In 1976, I nudged my sleeping college friend on his shoulder and whispered, "Paul, Paul, Dr. Haines is calling on you." With seismic force the stocky napper woke up and bolted to his feet. This was especially shocking since no one stood to answer questions—until now.

He was suddenly face-to-face with the brilliant and rather authoritarian Professor Haines—in his routine dark suit, pencil-thin tie and starched white shirt. The legendary Prof looked through his heavy oversized glasses while catching his breath, but the glitch was momentary and memorable.

The veteran professor gazed at this young disheveled student whose cockeyed glasses revealed his disorientation, not to mention Paul's shirt; it could have passed for a topographical map.

Dr. Haines, who had been mid-sentence in a discussion on the "Trinity," had little chance to respond before Paul blurted out:

"Dr. Haines, Sir...ugh, sorry, Sir. I had the answer on the tip of my tongue and lost it."

The brilliant professor gathered his wits, stared at the novice theologian, then declared:

"Young man, this is the saddest day in my teaching career. Scholars have been looking for the answer to the Trinity for centuries—and you had it on the tip of your tongue and lost it! Now sit down young man, and be quiet!"

I swallowed my fist to the elbow to keep from laughing.

Oftentimes, what comes quickly to our tongue reveals the depths or shallowness of our knowledge. Or, sleep deprivation. The above story is adapted from my account in *Straight Talk: Clear Answers about Today's Christianity*. I add to this account: "When the above story took place, I was a new Christian and had only recently learned the difference between the Old and New Testaments. Terms like '*Trinity*' and '*theology*' were not in my high school vocabulary. Even the main creed of Christianity, the 'Nicene Creed,' was new to me."

When people asked me questions, my naiveté and unfamiliarity revealed my lack of knowledge of the most basic religious elements. And my own questions also put me squarely among the biblical illiterates, e.g., "Were Abraham and Joseph disciples of Jesus?" I wasn't dumb, just uniformed.

And I knew even less about Judaism, Islam, other religions and the various cults. Besides a discussion with a then-state politician, the stately Tony Maidenberg, my first known conversation with a practicing Jew was when I arrived at the Tel Aviv airport to study for a semester in Jerusalem. Within hours, I found myself being thrown out of a convenient store for holding a slice of pepperoni pizza. The owner kept yelling "Not Kosher! Not Kosher!" and I sheepishly replied, "No, it's only pepperoni pizza." I was clueless. My first known conversation with a Muslim was with an American student seated next to me en route to Israel—and upon landing he was immediately greeted with harsh treatment due to his relatives' associations.

Many politicians have been caught off guard with basic facts, from a president telling Germans, "I am a bagel," to another president not knowing the capital of Poland. More recently, the indefatigable Sarah Palin ran into some knowledge issues during her now legendary interview with Katie Couric.

These sudden responses aren't just about one's knowledge base, from Jeopardy trivia to matters of State. At times they reveal one's moral and ethical compass.

The deeper we go spiritually, the more consistently we are spontaneously. And, the more principled we are in private the more prepared we are in public. When an unexpected question about a girl causes one's boyfriend to cough up his drink, there's a good chance he's guilty of something. When the politicians in Illinois gave evasive answers about selling a Senate seat, the American public smelled a rat. Spontaneous answers seem to alert various senses when something seems afoul.

My sister used this spontaneity angle in brilliant fashion with her one hundred employees. When she first took on her managerial duties she was informed that a few people slept during the work shift. She waited until they disappeared for an extended time, then went and placed a chair in that general area and waited to place a cell phone call. When they staggered around the corner and saw their boss, my sister, she'd catch them off guard and ask, "Hi _____, were you sleeping?" Without thinking and still waking up, they'd say something like, "Yeah, was sound asleep when the *&@! phone rang." And with much calculation, she'd respond, "Well, you can go home and catch up on your sleep; you're fired."

I was assisting with a youth program and was planning to recruit a businessman to mentor students. Quite accidentally and without his knowledge, I overheard a freckled middle school girl ask him in front of her friends, "Dr. So & So, I'm surprised you went to see Porky's II." He quickly responded, "Well, . . . I never would have gone had I known what it was about." Not aware that her brother worked the ticket booth, she responded. "Hmm. I figured after seeing Porky's I you would have known."

What kind of things do you say when startled from a deep sleep? And are your gaffes from a lack of knowledge or character? Sometimes neither is excusable, as our work and maturation levels expect higher standards. But true character stands the test of time, even if you find yourself standing unexpectedly.

Buck Creek Wisdom #36

"The deeper we go spiritually, the more consistently we are spontaneously."

"The more principled we are in private the more prepared we are in public."

"Spontaneous answers alert various senses when something seems afoul."

"It matters more what we do while awake than how long we avoid sleep."

Buck Creek & the Bible

The Bible has a trove of practical advice about slothful behavior, from the signposts of mundane tasks to wasted lives. "Through laziness, the rafters sag; because of idle hands, the house leaks." (Ecclesiastes 10:18) "A little sleep, a little slumber, a little folding of the hands to rest—and poverty will come on you like a thief and scarcity like an armed man." (Proverbs 24:33-34)

"All hard work brings a profit, but mere talk leads only to poverty." (Proverbs 14:23)

CHAPTER THIRTY-SEVEN:
Stealing Pop and Smashing Pears

The Snookie from our era—and each childhood had one—was a pre-GED twenty-something named Big John. For the Snookies of our lives, scruples aren't optional they're merely absent. Snookies brashly suck the life out of others while magnifying their own ephemeral needs. Snookies promote Swiss cheese social filters with a smile and sometimes cleavage.

Big John didn't bare his chest but his pseudo-confidence. One dark night I heard him whisper to younger boys, "If you open the bottle while it's still in the machine, and then lean the pop machine forward, it's free!" And presto—it was! He instructed his streetwise protégés as they poured (leaned) half a cup of an *Orange Crush*. They made it about half way down the vertical row of bottles before the tilt was too much.

The Buck Creek storeowner installed more lights. Stretched fishing string with cans in the alley. Put marbles atop the machine. Our Snookie man-child relentlessly persuaded boys to steal pop they really didn't want.

I only went once, tagging along as a junior higher, but later heard about the last time the Snookie-ites ventured into "Old Man Jeffery's" store lot.

Just as they were about to tip the machine, "Boom!!" They scampered behind the few trees next to the train tracks. "The old man has gone loony!" They had really irritated him and thought they had won. They got their courage again, waited for his back door to shut, and following Big John's orders, started toward the machine again. "Boom! Boom!!" Screaming ensued. "I've been shot. Oh my God! The old man shot me! He shot me!" the story goes.

Mr. Jeffery had tricked them, slamming the back door and going immediately out the front and sneaking back around.

Using rock salt, he peppered those trees with crystal pellets and barely hit Rob—the screamer. For the rest of the school year, Rob's colleagues would shout down the hallways, "I've been shot! Oh my God! The old man shot me! He shot me!"

Someone usually staggered around performing a Dick Van Dyke type of over-exaggeration and then *thud*; he'd hit the floor and give some final dying request. "Please tell Auntie Em I'll miss her." Or, "Tell her I love her; tell my sweet Connie (Rob's girlfriend) that Steve (the acting victim) will take care of her." Oh, we'd laugh at these stories. We'd snicker 'til the cows came home, or until Rob came near.

Stealing pop was a challenge that soon lost its luster. Mr. Jeffery's store eventually went out of business, Big John finally took a generic job in another state, and pop machines with bottles became a thing of the past. But Buck Creek wasn't an anomaly, nor is today's fascination with Snookies.

Through the centuries, people have done dastardly and self-centered public deeds just for the sake of doing them, as noted by the great St. Augustine. He admits of such actions before his conversion to Christianity—recorded in his biographical devotional, *Confessions* (A.D. 397). He joined some teen friends and stole pears from an old man's orchard—then smashed them. Fruit trees were rather important resources in that era, and in a sense, like stealing from Mr. Jeffery, Augustine was stealing his elderly neighbor's livelihood.

Augustine tells the story to help us understand our sinful behavior as fallen human beings (fallen from our created state in the Garden of Eden, according to the Bible, through the sin of Adam and Eve). Augustine realizes that he did this act for no other motivation than for the thrill of sinning—stealing for stealing's sake. In a sense, he recognizes a Snookie in all of us that needs controlled. Smashing pears was perhaps his perverse way of trying to demonstrate power over the God that created him, exercising freedom for wrongdoing, just to do it. He recognizes the realities of social pressures on individual acts, and that some social groups can work towards uplifting and good behavior and others toward destructive acts. He finds no quick solution to this tension within us—but suggests there's hope to overcome it.

And this intersects with parents and social planners, and the need for moral education as well. We need to give liberally to Boys and Girls Clubs, the YM- and WYCA, Boy and Girl Scouts, and youth groups of our houses of faith. We should likewise demand excellence from institutions such as K-12 schools and higher education.

I was livid a few years ago when one of our university's recent graduates reported to his first day of student teaching dressed in a tie, only to be greeted by a veteran teacher wearing an AC/DC t-shirt. I wondered if Big John had schemed his way into teaching; certainly a principal wouldn't overlook the need for role models among such impressionable teens.

They don't tip pop machines anymore. However, teens today tip computers for "free" downloads and dwell on Snookie YouTube clips. These are but a few of the sad manifestations of our individual fallenness accented by today's open-source norms.

The next time a teen smashes a modern-day pear, remember it's not generational but reflective of our human condition.

Snookies aren't named for one random act in life, or we'd all be so named, but for being applauded and encouraged into a lifestyle, and all the while choosing to smile.

Buck Creek Wisdom #37

"Assisting sinister leaders isn't being cooperative but complicit."

"There are no ethical grey areas as visceral decisions should be guilt free."

"Darkness never masks sin from Light."

Buck Creek & the Bible

The metaphor of darkness is used in different ways. In the following passage, Jesus uses it in reference to a fuller understanding of his promises: "I am the light of the world. Whoever follows me will never walk in darkness, but will have the light of life." (John 8:12) Through Apostle Paul, we are indeed instructed to focus on this same "light," on truth revealed through Christ and his message, and the positive aspects of God's creation: "Finally, brothers and sisters, whatever is true, whatever is noble, whatever is right, whatever is pure, whatever is lovely, whatever is admirable—if anything is excellent or praiseworthy—think about such things." (Philippians 4:8)

Dr. Jerry Pattengale

CHAPTER THIRTY-EIGHT:
Swimming the Wrong Race

I thought I had won the freestyle race at the all-school swim meet, beating one of the state's fastest swimmers—then they told me I was supposed to be doing the butterfly!

Those were jeers not cheers, brutal sarcastic yells. To make matters worse, I barely won. I shared Phil Mickelson's infamous statement thirty years before he said it on camera after blowing a tournament—"I'm an idiot!" In both cases, we were embarrassed. You're no more alone and defenseless than being a spindly-legged, hollow–chested, porcelain-skinned, scraggly-haired, undersized teen dripping wet in hand-me-down shorts in front of your high school peers.

Rules make all the difference. Although not much of a consolation, my Buck Creek peers realized I simply had made an honest mistake. But the rub today is people making dishonest ones.

The lines are blurred between shame, guilt and embarrassment. Two years ago the nation read about the dishonest accountant at our son's school. He embezzled a mountain of money—in front of bankers, lawyers, and over two hundred students whose school

169

suddenly had to deal with the staggering loss. Many national media outlets covered the story—especially one brazen expenditure: a seven hundred dollar vasectomy the accountant charged on the organization's credit card, then submitted the receipt for a second reimbursement (healthcare).

During the four years of rampant personal spending of the school's funds he began driving a parade of new cars, he also chromed a Harley, and made lifestyle choices that didn't fit his budget. Our teen son perhaps showed more wisdom than us adults during those years. He approached the accountant on a few occasions after seeing him in new wheels, and asked, "Hey, nice ride. Are you dipping into the offering plate?" Or, "So that's where our tuition is going?"

It's sad, but the county's best-performing high school didn't survive his embezzlement.

Around the same time, Nasdaq's chairman Bernie Madoff was indicted for a Ponzi scheme, which bilked eight thousand investors of over fifty billion dollars. Like our school's accountant, the questions of guilt, shame and embarrassment came to the forefront. While our penal system prorates punishment on the size of infraction, our curiosity wonders as much about the first dollars swindled as the last several. At what point did the school accountant go from a simple (honest?) mistake, to realizing the possibility to repeat it, to living with the reality that he was jeopardizing an entire school? Or, when did Madoff—already highly successful financially by most standards—begin to feel at ease ripping off friends?

In D.C., I heard classical scholar Victor Davis Hanson (Stanford) note that Western society has lost its sense of shame—the strongest of the defenses against such avarice and corruption. His positions on related subjects are accessible through his weekly column for National Review Online and his thrice-weekly blog for Pajamas Media, "Work and Days," along with his seventeen books.

Using his classical sources, I'm reminded of the Athenian practice of "ostracizing" politicians. The word derives from the Greek for potshard (*ostracon*—clay fragment from a broken pot). The Athenians would vote annually on shards, and if a politician ever received the majority of votes (with at least six thousand minimum cast for all politicians of public figures) he or she would be banished to the Black Sea area for ten years. This sense of public shame was intended to thwart corruption and damage to the democratic culture. While ostracism in classical Greece was not a trial or declaration of guilt, it was all the same very public—an ultimate opinion poll with consequences.

Yeah, I thought I had won the race in the pool—but competed by the wrong set of rules. And, it was my last public race. I realized I had Titanic buoyancy and escargot-like speed. At some point, I realized both my "birthright gifts" along with the areas of my "honed skills"—categories popularized by Parker Palmer (author of *Courage to Teach*). Creativity was among the former, writing and editing skills among the latter. No matter how creative I got, I would never have increased my swimming speed without cheating. No matter how articulate I became in describing my swimming, no medals were in the making. For Madoff, he was much closer to his birthright gifts and honed skills, which makes his crime all the more detestable—clearly aware of not only the dishonesty and vacuous ethics, but ruin to institutions and trusting individuals. Our school accountant, the same. There were other honest routes to acquiring wealth with his gifts, but he chose shortcuts that cut the hearts out of a trusting community.

Both Madoff and our accountant are being ostracized, but in the modern sense of the word. They've been incarcerated not simply for our protection, but through the justice of a trial system. I don't know Madoff, but feel for Kevin Bacon and Spielberg and the 7,998 others he bilked. I do know the accountant—a likeable fellow—but hurt for those great kids he swindled. I've learned long ago to make decisions on principle not personality—the principle mandates a guilty vote.

When I stood on the pool's edge, my classmates' view of my personality wasn't the issue. Playing by the rules was. The next time you watch a clip of Michael Phelps winning the gold, imagine yourself winning. Then run the same dream without using a rowboat.

Buck Creek Wisdom #38

"Healthy societies begin to wane upon losing their sense of shame."

"A convicted thief with a price is still a thief."

"Honed skills should buttress our birthright gifts instead of becoming our careers."

Buck Creek & the Bible

"Whoever of you loves life and desires to see many good days, keep your tongue from evil and your lips from telling lies. Turn from evil and do good; seek peace and pursue it. The eyes of the Lord are on the righteous, and his ears are attentive to their cry; but the face of the Lord is against those who do evil, to blot out their name from the earth." (Psalm 34: 12-16)

CHAPTER THIRTY-NINE:
Worms in Square Knots at Blue Heron Lake

My friend Rod Crossman has a laugh that swallows Arkansas. He tilts back and twists that long body while sucking in part of the ozone layer. Nothing excites him more than fishing stories—especially true ones that involve his friends. In fact, he's become internationally recognized for his paintings of fishing scenes. Well, I doubt he'll ever paint the following story—but he might tilt and twist a bit.

Just north of Marion, Indiana is the serene Blue Heron Lake, once hidden from the world and the site of a memorable fishing excursion with a group of teen boys.

Remember, I was born in Buck Creek, Indiana and walked creek beds daily, selling soft crawls for two cents and hard shells for a penny. I've "noodled" with uncles on the Tippy and Wabash Rivers, dam fished with huge weights, ganged up on Walleye for a few years on Lake Erie and caught two buckets of catfish on a can and string pole at Ken Heer's Lake Webster Cottage. Even took New York subways with teens to go crabbing at Coney Island. At Camp Tecumseh in Brookston, Indiana, I caught two sixteen-inch largemouth bass on the opposite ends of the same lure.

As a teen, I once followed a well-supplied professional fisherman back Sugar Creek to a hidden nook where a huge bass got away. He cursed and immediately left, but I returned to catch the monster—an eighteen-inch smallmouth bass (on a night crawler and a cheap Zebco 202!).

But all that didn't prepare me for a night at Blue Heron.

I took a dozen teens on a camping trip from our newly formed youth program, the J.C. Body Shop. A couple had never been fishing. Todd was especially gullible even though he had just aced the SAT as a sophomore. He once shot a thirty-six on one golf hole because his "friends," Todd and Greg, told him he had "to play it where it lied." Yep, "lied" was about right. He said, "Mr. Pattengale, I thought I'd never get out of that pond!"

At Blue Heron Lake (then called Phillipee's Place), I noticed many were catching frogs on the south side of the pond, while across the way sat Todd, alone, determined to catch the big one. His pole was completely bent. "Todd, I think you have something! Pull it! Hurry, yank it!" He calmly responded, "Oh, no, Mr. Pattengale, that's just the special bait I'm using." It was as if I had a lobotomy scar and fishing was new—and he was dead serious.

"Well, Todd, let me see that special bait you have on your hook." He reeled in one of the largest river weights I've ever seen, pole bending all the while, and then lifted it and shared, "Oh, no, Mr. Pattengale. You don't need a hook with this special bait. You see, the fish come along and smell this, then swallow it. Then, you just reel them in!"

Stunned by this nonsense and simultaneously amused at his naiveté, I could hardly respond without overreacting. "Todd, about how long have you been using this special bait?" "Oh, Mr. Pattengale, only about an hour." I prodded, "And how many bites have you had?" With the emotion of a rock he responded in full belief, "Oh, none—but Greg and Jeff told me it takes about an hour, and then they just can't stand it any more and a lot will come."

Interrupting his friends' frog expedition to scold them—another shock! These novice froggers were cooking frog legs on top of lanterns! After canceling their pseudo-Epicurean snack and likely paint poisoning from Coleman steel, I sent Greg and Jeff over to inform Todd of fishing realities. With smirks on their faces they sheepishly followed their flashlights back to Todd and his bent pole and allegedly explained hooks and worms.

Later from my smores' campfire spot I noticed Todd repeatedly casting. Upon advising him to have patience, he noted: "Oh, I let the worm have time to get the fish's attention, then reel back in to make sure the knot is tight." This time it wasn't a heavy weight but a bare hook. He reached in to a nearly empty worm carton, grabbed a night crawler, and proceeded to tie it on the hook.

"You know, Mr. Pattengale, it's very difficult to tie some of these smaller ones in a square knot. They squirm quite a bit." Once again, I scratched my head and asked him why he didn't put the hook through them. "Oh, no, Mr. Pattengale, that would kill the worm. Greg and Jeff told me never to do that, but to tie them tight so they'd stay on and wiggle for the fish to see."

Needless to say, Todd never caught a fish that night, and to my knowledge, any night. But he managed to catch a few lessons. And, I'm happy to say that all of these boys turned out fine—though likely won't be appearing with Bill Dance or Bill Rock anytime soon.

And for you anglers who want a slice of heaven, which Rod Crossman calls fly fishing, you might check out his award-winning paintings: www.rodcrossman.com. We've had one hanging in our entryway for nearly thirty years and purchased it not long after a few worms slipped their square knots.

Buck Creek Wisdom #39

"In order to get a bite you need to have a line in the water."

"Campfires have a way of casting our intellect's shadow."

"Bait without a hook is pointless and a hook without bait is fruitless."

Buck Creek & the Bible

We are charged to take action, to be "proactive" instead of remaining passive: "Go to the ant, you sluggard; consider its ways and be wise! It has no commander, no overseer or ruler, yet it stores its provisions in summer and gathers its food at harvest." (Proverbs 6:6-8)

Dr. Jerry Pattengale

CHAPTER FORTY:
Fast and Furious: Wrong Turns with No Return

I spent a year in the theater one day. Franklin and Eric, our "adopted" Chinese sons, invited me to *Fast and Furious*. I grew up around racecars and swearing, but that date seemed like a barrage of counter-intuitive physics and a grammar lesson on grunge multisyllabic expletives. I could have inhaled a bottle of Anacin through a straw by the movie's end and still had a headache. Flippant deaths and triple flipped cars crush sensibilities. I didn't know whether to ask for my money back, borrow rosary beads, or reach for Pepto-Bismol.

I've witnessed a senseless death among fast cars, the night the races never got on track. The flagman made a fatal mistake after he started my dad's stockcar race—he turned right instead of left. The woman two seats from me bolted up and released a shrieking scream that still echoes forty years later. Bulging veins in her temple. Breathless gasping between sobs. A friend clutching her. Like a scene from *Psycho* that never leaves you, her despair still reaches through the decades.

We all quickly learned that those clothes stuck in the open left wheel well of the 1965 Chevy were her husband's, and he was still wearing them.

It was surrealistic. They looked like loose pajamas, nothing more, and most of us hadn't actually seen the accident. I recall watching him climbing down from the tower as my dad's car passed, and I followed him a bit. My dad was a brilliant mechanic but a terrible racecar driver. He usually had a few too many Falls City beers before the race, becoming lethargic on the track. This particular night, the flagman apparently also had imbibed and lost his sense of direction.

Ironically, he started a race that finished his.

We make decisions daily, and often it's the routine that dulls our judgment. Just as great things and heroic stories often have origins in common settings, so do grave mistakes and premature endings.

The flagman would have been a grandparent today, perhaps a great-grandfather as well. I wonder what his children tell their kids about his death. "He was a good man, but one day he turned right instead of left."

Several years ago, my wife gave me instructions before I headed to Greece for eight weeks with the National Endowment for the Humanities. She said, "Promise me that you'll not do anything that puts your life in danger; our sons have already lost one dad." He had been killed by an unprovoked random act of an unknown drunken teenager when their three boys were under five years old—now our three oldest sons (in college and beyond). I promised. The day came when the team went to a site known for cliff diving. Besides a token, medium-height, foot-first cowardly jump, I passed when they went to higher cliffs.

I've always loved adventure, and the challenge and thrill were there for the taking—but I had promised and passed. I must admit, the height was rather daunting, and it looked like they were jumping into a thimble.

On another occasion I was speaking at Lake Arrowhead outside of Los Angeles, and the collegians asked me to go rock climbing. I happened to know that the cliff was named "Suicide Hill" and that their favorite climber had recently died from a fall. I passed.

Well, I've made my share of life-threatening decisions, from eating too much red meat to drinking gallons with NutraSweet, but overall I've tried not to live on the edge (though golfing with my friends Jess and John nearly qualifies). I want to live long, to watch our kids marry and have our grandkids, and to observe as they pursue what God has for them.

Of all things, I don't want to put myself in a place where I might turn right when I need to turn left, and prematurely leave for good. My dad turned right instead of left, but his step was a long one, inched through a lifetime of long-necked beer bottles and filterless smokes. And what seemed just as suddenly as clothes in a wheel well, we were staring at a backless suit in a bargain coffin.

Yes, I want to live fully, mainly for our four boys and their kids. I've been tickled recently seeing billboards in our hometown with folks in their eighties having fun. The big phrase reads, "They got their Sizzle back!" Pictured on horses to skateboards, these people look like they're indeed sizzling. I called the company (TLC Management) and learned that those pictured are actual residents! I'll drive out of my way just to see those billboard smiles. Ingenious promotion—resonating with our human condition and helping us to smile while hoping.

Yeah, I want to live fully for our sons and daughters-in-law. For new programs at church. For concerts and pottery shows. For Little League games with jerseys sporting our family name. For our town. For my elderly friends in the country. For books yet to be written, and others yet to be read.

Peter Marshall said it's not our duration in life that matters, but our donation. Living fully is more about the latter, but I'd sure like to do it a long time.

I don't want to turn right instead of left, but rather with an eye for what's right and what's left to do.

Buck Creek Wisdom #40

"It's not our duration in life that matters,
but our donation." (Peter Marshall)

"Finding life direction involves keeping an eye
for what's right and what's left to do."

"Bucket lists and kicking the bucket should
not be a cause and effect."

Buck Creek & the Bible

"Whatever your hand finds to do, do it with all your might, for in the realm of the dead, where you are going, there is neither working nor planning nor knowledge nor wisdom." (Ecclesiastes 9:10)

CHAPTER FORTY-ONE:
The Lesson of Red Ryders

About the only thing that hurt worse than taking a BB in the lip was getting snagged in the neck by my cousin's fishhook. I suppose we can chalk up the first to adolescent foolishness and the second to bad timing, but either way it's amazing what we endure for fun.

In the simple Indiana cemetery on a knoll near a whiteboard church, we boys of Buck Creek met for our annual BB gun fight. It was my first at thirteen-years-old. A backwoods areligious bar mitzvah of sorts.

We wore more clothes than during the urban Izod craze of the early 80s. Old WWII and Nam helmets, ski hats, goggles, mouth pieces, cups, extra socks and coats—all in the August heat. But I still felt naked when suddenly pinned against Mr. Kaufmann's large tombstone.

My former neighbor's granite shrine only served to ricochet the tiny metal sorties. Three Skoal-breath seniors stood over me and took more shots than Allen Iverson. I felt like Mr. Bill in a hailstorm and squealed more than my cousin getting shot by a potato gun from twenty feet.

They pummeled me from the chest down, and my shins especially stung. The rule was that one hit above the waist eliminated you from the game, but they weren't about to end their fun prematurely.

Then my cousin Bruce appeared like a superhero. His ambush worked, at least momentarily. It was pretty funny until an errant shot hit somewhere on the granite around "Kaufmann" and then found my lower lip. Someone raised the white flag (some old briefs), and the seniors had me swear not to tell my parents about the pseudo-Red Ryder rumble. Then they carted me aside while they finished the game.

I recalled that story last year as my friend John Blake shared about his welts from playing paintball with his kids and grandkids. During the game, he had been hit, walked out with hands raised only to be nailed while in this vulnerable stance. While paintballing is reportedly safe, forty-nine-dollar Red Ryders seem archaic and less threatening next to the eight-hundred-dollar Tippmann A5 paintball guns that can give you a facelift from fifty feet, or an Ariakon Pro Elite that can send you to Hair Club for Men if you lose your hat.

I'm not sure what prompted my golfing buddy to go into the woods against these highly skilled and tech savvy Millennial militia. Perhaps it was a "Bucket List" thing? Nonetheless, Blake's a great dad and grandfather and a wounded one at that.

We live in a free country where men can be boys and boys can play men. Some games make little sense to those of us more fragile types. And others, like ice fishing, seem about as inviting as a Rosanne Barr National Anthem rerun.

But we need to keep perspective. While we run through the woods as boys of summer, our neighbor's son drives through Iraq in a targeted Hummer. While we watch glib movies and spend hours on the Wii, our relatives are trekking through Afghanistan helping others to be free.

Yes, we did stupid things in our youth and by the grace of God can smile at our folly. And while we hope for our young sons to avoid such carelessness, we pray the same for our older sons' safety (and for the protection of their elders—us).

There may come a day when we think the only recourse is to raise our arms in surrender, but history tells us that others aren't as forgiving as our American ideals dictate. The Assyrians conquered countries like ancient Israel and routinely exported their inhabitants, replacing them with their own. The Scythians from the Russian Steppes decapitated victims and drank from their skulls. The Romans exacted substantial tributes. The Mayans buried entire civilizations. The Nazis incinerated them. Rwandans dismembered even the little children. Hussein's Iraq endorsed inhumane punishments.

And the list will continue as long as humans without the love of God continue to act unchecked out of their depravity. Iran openly threatens to obliterate Israel. The Koran explicitly calls for violence against Christians and other non-believing (non-Muslim) populations. Juarez, Mexico is riddled with thousands of slaughter stains from recent drug-related slayings—literally in the shadow of a great American institution of higher learning, UTEP.

Yes, it was irrational to have BB gun fights in Buck Creek, risking blindness, dental repair and swollen lips. Kids seem to do a lot of irrational things, but unfortunately they don't have the corner on that market. While UTEP and six thousand other American universities teach justice and civility, reprobate segments and sects continue to give reason for the very existence of such colleges.

No matter how fervently we preach openness and tolerance, history shows that humans are not all on the same page. Our fallen nature is especially pronounced and unchecked in some sinister groups exhausting themselves to close the book on America's freedom.

Diplomacy, no matter how articulate and well meaning, will never eradicate violence. Several millennia of human history testify to this.

And if our educational courses work, violence will never eradicate attempts of diplomacy.

Unless human nature changes for the first time since Adam and Eve, the ultimate protection of ideals and the only guarantee of diplomacy will remain a strong military. Ideas have consequences—ideals. Some demand destruction and others diplomacy. Both philosophies necessitate guns much larger than Red Ryders.

Buck Creek Wisdom #41

"One's rejection of the truth does not nullify the truth."

"Articulate and well-meaning diplomacy will never eradicate violence. And if our educational courses work, violence will never eradicate attempts of diplomacy."

"Ideas have consequences called ideals; some demand destruction and others diplomacy."

Buck Creek & the Bible

Some situations have rather clear biblical guidance, such as the following command: "Rescue those being led away to death; hold back those staggering toward slaughter." (Proverbs 24:11) However, for those living under oppressive regimes other Scripture seems to place such "clear" advice in tension, e.g., "Submit yourselves for the Lord's sake to every human authority: whether to the emperor, as the supreme authority, or to governors, who are sent by him to punish those who do wrong and to commend those who do right. For it is God's will that by doing good you should silence the ignorant talk of foolish people. Live as free people, but do not use your freedom as a cover-up for evil; live as God's slaves. Show proper respect to everyone, love the family of believers, fear God, honor the emperor." (1 Peter 2:13-17) Large groups of Christians have become Pacifists, others imbibe a "Just War" theory. Self-defense and protecting others' lives, and various related issues, evoke a wide range of responses. Even one of the Ten Commandments has qualifiers, i.e., "Thou shall not kill" (Exodus 20:13). Yep, the punishment is being stoned (Leviticus 24:16-17).

Dr. Jerry Pattengale

CHAPTER FORTY-TWO:
No More Tiptoeing through Human Trafficking

Watching Tiny Tim's striptease version of "Tiptoe through the Tulips" seemed to reveal an eclectic flower missing some petals.

It's a picture I wish hadn't been painted. The frilly tux shirt flew into the crowd and his shoes hit the wall while his stretchy black pants were tugged from his hairy snow cone legs.

A pear-shaped, black-haired Winnie the Pooh in oversized fuchsia satin briefs and cheap black dress socks strutted effeminately through makeshift tulips. Women pretended not to look but kept peeking from behind their hands. Inebriated men were screaming, "Hold me back, Honey!" Some threw dollar-bill insults.

Energy filled the place. Near pandemonium ensued. Profits grew! The hotel manager was happy and Tim's agent surely smiled from his distant den.

Tiny Tim gave his patented over-the-shoulder flick of his long curly hair, rolled his mascara eyes, and strummed his ukulele one last time.

A few hours earlier, I took a room service order to him, which changed my view of his act on the stage of despair.

A greasy-haired, overweight, aloof celebrity talked to me in a canary voice with a twinge of Edith Bunker.

He took my pen with his curly fingernails and signed his bill for an odd order: three bottles of catsup, three jars of mustard, two baskets of club crackers and a six pack of club soda. Not normal, especially for a cast member from *You Are What You Eat*.

At fifteen years old, I was staring deep life issues in the face—albeit with a quirky profile. I later learned from an NPR interview that his scary white makeup helped him feel pure instead of unattractive.

I realized that behind the eccentric persona was a hurting disheveled middle-aged man. He wasn't just performing at bars but was imprisoned by financial realities.

Tiny Tim admitted he drew attention but no followers and confidants—a recipe for loneliness.

There on the outskirts of Lafayette, Indiana not far from my childhood romps of Battle Ground and Buck Creek, was a man wishing for childhood friends like those listening to his *Little People* albums—people he could trust.

Not-so-Tiny-Tim shared his despair over greedy managers. All TV appearance checks, song royalties, and endorsements were gone—mainly to others. This included his estranged wife "Miss Vicki" whom he had married on the Tonight Show before forty million viewers. Now, in near obscurity, he enjoyed only ten percent of his take, and that couldn't be much. No big marquee, no big deal. He hadn't even made the banquet room venue. He was at the Holiday Inn lounge near Buck Creek, Indiana, a long way from Las Vegas.

We could have chatted for hours. Holding a thick discolored Bible, he outlined his oppressive, depressed existence and torturous absence from his daughter, Victoria Tulip.

Later that night, I watched this hurting, gentle human masquerade behind a vibrato repertoire. This Lebanese-Jewish musical genius no longer played to friendly crowds as a novelty act but to a contract as a freakish falsetto stripper.

The sweat-soaked, pride-spent man-child gathered his clothes, a few insulting dollars, and disappeared from the cheap orange-candled room for another second-bill bar, and within a couple years would become a circus act.

I had just witnessed the disconnection between public gyrations and a personal groaning for hope. He was prostituting himself—feeling strapped by life's turns and others' terms.

He's joined by a host of citizens and immigrants conscripted through coercion, trading self worth for warmth and sustenance, strutting in personal pain masked by the moment—selling from personal bleakness to human weakness. Unfortunately, it's symptomatic of a global pandemic even more dire—human trafficking.

My wife and I listened intently as Kristin Wiebe discussed World Hope International's anti-trafficking efforts, addressing an international crisis built on the same sinister notions that coerce stripteases and child porn. Her recent travels through Indonesia and Africa had seared memories of horrific child-prostitution and force-labor accounts—including children sold into frontline war duties, little girls sold by aunts to foreign pimps and displaced children unfamiliar with recess and recourse.

Her accounts reflect recent international reports. The United Nation's International Labor Organization estimates that 12.3 million people are currently in some form of forced labor.

At the very end of that Tiny Tim evening, only the regulars remained. It was a nightly tradition for our host to close with "People, Who Need People, Are The Luckiest People . . ." He carried a tulip to the stage, but sang the song with his usual grace and sincerity.

I leaned on a linen cart wondering what happens when a Tiny Tim knows this tune but finds no chorus—no people to help?

Somewhere in the night, in an aging van with a greedy agent's lackey at the wheel was a washed-up ukulele player who knew the song's message all too well.

And somewhere every night are human slaves that need people—not paying strangers, but strangers paying attention.

Tiny Tim eventually broke some of his shackles and even regained some sense of novelty fame, marrying his third wife on Jay Leno's *Tonight Show*. He died Nov. 30, 1996 from a heart attack while singing "Tiptoe" at a benefit for women.

Tiny Tim gave me a glimpse into the soul of humanity and an educational gaze at the harm some do to others. Uniqueness doesn't preclude goodness; a lesson, like my child-man friend, not easily forgotten.

Buck Creek Wisdom #42

"In some sense, we all stand naked before our peers."

"Uniqueness and strangeness do not preclude the capacity for goodness."

"The only social contract we're bound to is the one we follow."

Buck Creek & the Bible

"Rescue the weak and the needy; deliver them from the hand of the wicked." (Psalm 82:4)

Dr. Jerry Pattengale

CHAPTER FORTY-THREE:
Waving at Ayn Rand with Tube Socks on Your Hands

Changing your car's clutch plate in the snow means you're short on dough. I held the flashlight until my hands went numb. Double tube socks made for poor mittens. Dad's gloves went on and off until shortly before the sun arose and the car worked and so did he.

I spent a week in the windy snow that night. Dad would light another cigarette, swear a bit, and then slide back beneath the motor on his worn cardboard. A few jaunts into the house. A few hot chocolates and Falls City beers. More smokes and swear words. Then more cocoa and lame Chock Full o'Nuts. But somehow the night passed, and we survived another poor man's crisis.

Snow on the car's roof along with frosted windows branded those of us in rental houses at sunrise. Garages were status symbols. We likely burned an extra oil field just warming cars in the morning.

I wondered how many teens had to awaken during bitter Indiana nights to ensure the portable heat lamp under the hood was still burning. Or how many had to start the car every hour? How many understood the travesty of "a cracked block?" How many stacked bales of straw around their house's foundation? Put blankets over their upstairs doorways and moved everyone downstairs to save heat bills? Rode frigid school buses for an hour each morning?

But we survived; Buck Creek lives on and so do we. Though many didn't finish high school and only a few managed college, we collectively learned the value of a dollar—and its absence. The cold winters always pass. A few still slide on cardboard in sub-zero weather. A few are still finding themselves. A few die young.

My dad was a rapper three decades before the genre's time, but all in expletives. Manual labor, teen marriage, eight kids, no diploma, rattling cars, leaky roofs, and a litany of other reasons for his early heart attack. And, mountains of hops in bottles.

Like Ayn Rand's fictitious John Galt, my dad was a garage mechanic. I also left home at a young age for a conservative college (Indiana Wesleyan, instead of Patrick Henry). And thirty years later I, too, am worried about burgeoning bureaucracies and Galt's prediction of "collectivist government" collapsing.

But in the 1970s in Buck Creek, there were no John Galts. None of my hundreds of relatives sat around discussing the plot of Rand's opus, *Atlas Shrugged* (1957). There was no talk of "Galt's Gulch," or establishing the remote backwater town as Indiana's version of Rand's counter to egalitarians.

Rand's novel creatively captures the advantages of free enterprise, limited government and individual rights; she produced a brilliantly provocative tome behind only the Bible in sales last decade. However, her overall life philosophy doesn't square with the reality of the human condition. In her famous 1964 *Playboy* interview she explicitly notes that man is not to be held accountable for actions that are his nature (original sin). Also, that man's "own happiness is his highest moral purpose." She promotes egoism. In the end, that's what led to my father's undoing and abandonment of our family—not poverty. What happens with the notion of responsibility and civility in Rand's personal philosophy?

Rand exclaims: "Man—every man—is an end in himself, not the means to the ends of others. He must exist for his own sake, neither sacrificing himself to others nor sacrificing others to himself. The pursuit of his own rational self-interest and of his own happiness is the highest moral purpose of his life."

The release of *Goddess of the Market: Ayn Rand and the American Right* (Oxford, 2009), prompted provocative responses by Gary

Moore, "Ayn Rand: Goddess of the Great Recession" *(Christianity Today,* 9/2010) and "Wall Street Anti-Christ?" (YouTube). His subtitle tips his hand—"Why Christians should be wary of the late pop philosopher and her disciples." He unveils the fallacy of Randian views that excuse businesses of any social responsibility except "to make money." Rand flaunted her "selfishness" tenet by wearing dollar-sign broaches, which Moore reminds us symbolized its blatant anti-Christian substitution for the cross.

Her casket sported a wreath in the shape of a dollar sign, and looking on was her star pupil, Alan Greenspan. Her beliefs are on display in the *Atlas* film trilogy (2011).

Moore calls for "a more ethical, prudent approach," not a Randian one that could actually endorse the avarice on Wall Street. He also highlights the fallacy of businesses' true financial independence, especially in a season of bailouts.

Rand's amoral philosophy is diametrically opposed to the agenda of the Business Civic Leadership Center (the U.S. Chamber of Commerce) and Amy Sherman's work on charitable choice (*Kingdom Calling: Vocational Stewardship for the Common Good* [2011]). Her advocacy of community renewal is in stark contrast to Rand's maxim that "charity is not a moral duty."

We survive amazing challenges. And if truth indeed matches reality, fulfillment comes from more than possessions and financial success. Rand herself had the inner tension of being depressed because she couldn't be the perfect "man" she created—even with wealth.

Regardless of our challenges or comfort levels, whether working on cars in the snow or weathering the elements in a luxury sedan, the cold passes and we usually live for another season. While Rand makes reason the absolute, we need to be more concerned with the reason we look for absolutes.

The next time you see a cold boy with tube socks on his hands, lend him a hand—unless you think it's possible not to see it as your moral duty.

Buck Creek Wisdom #43

"Truth matches reality."

"Before making reason the absolute consider the reason we seek absolutes."

"In order to thrive we must first survive."

"The belief that man is the end-all explains why so many men try to end it all."

"Flaunting dollar signs symbolizes the worst kind of bankruptcy."

Buck Creek & the Bible

"Do nothing out of selfish ambition or vain conceit. Rather, in humility value others above yourselves, not looking to your own interests but each of you to the interests of the others." (Philippians 2:3-4)

CHAPTER FORTY-FOUR:
Naked Ned and Catastrophes

Ned snuck back into Buck Creek, from tree to tree and slithering through ditches. He was naked.

In the 1970s, hazing was the norm. The seniors had dropped poor, skinny Ned about a mile from town—after wrestling him from his Wranglers. No Brett Favre denim look, but more of a gaunt Don Knotts' appeal. One minute he thought he was finally part of the gang, and another minute he was an exclamation mark on embarrassment.

It wasn't like he could hitchhike home.

Imagine a carload of guys seeing him in their headlights—they'd pelt him with their Buds and Pabst Blue Ribbons. Or an elderly couple—they'd yell "Pervert!" then honk all the way home. Or worst, a carload of girls—they'd whistle, make sarcastic observations, offer him a ride and then speed off as he got near.

What excuses could Ned use? "Oh, I was auditioning for Adam in the school play, and my car died." Or, "Clothes? . . . Oh my; I thought I was forgetting something." In the 21st-century, law suits fly over hazing. In the 1970s, birthday suit scenes were rituals.

The only consolation for Ned was that he was among many who had made that naked trek back to town. It was in jest, no harm intended. In fact, embarrassment was about the extent of the damage (perhaps joined by lifelong therapy).

Fortunately, hazing is no longer allowed. Unfortunately, many kids endure much more serious treatment.

In 2008, I joined the shocked crowds around giant airport flat screens. I had just heard the riveting testimony of Dr. Jo Anne Lyon, founding president of World Hope International (and now the top official in the Wesleyan denomination). Dr. Lyon had shared horrific stories about slave trafficking in developing countries, and rampant poverty and diseases—often linked to political greed and disregard for human casualties. The actions in places far away seemed horrific but distant, places outside the civilized west and beyond the reaches of technological advances and high culture.

Against this backdrop, the plasma screens displayed disturbing images from a homemade Austrian dungeon. It was a bunker where Josef Fritzl imprisoned his own daughter for twenty-four years beneath his family's condo, and sired seven kids with her. Austria (bordering Germany) is within the cradle of European advancement; it's not a developing country where much of the human trafficking and rapacious actions were being reported. The region's educational model has long since dominated American research institutes and colleges in general (the "German model").

In the midst of the quaint town of Amstetten, Fritzl had lured his daughter into a subterranean room constructed to detain her for his continued sexual pleasure—for twenty-four years! At seventy-three years old, Fritzl was a living reminder of the need for laws, moral codes, and child protection agencies. The need for places like Marion Family Services and for prosecutors like Jim Luttrull, Jr. (Grant County, Indiana, with a national reputation for work against pedophiles)—exhausting themselves on behalf of abused children.

Sadly, every town (including my own) has accounts of sinful elders violating youthful innocence. Beyond the repeated rapes and assaults, and confining his grandchildren sired through his own daughter for their entire lives, Fritzl was numb to the daily routine. For most civilized moral folks it's unfathomable to think of such actions, let alone years of digging up one's basement under darkness and running a secretive routine of rape and oppression by day. Inconceivable.

The local paper in hometowns across America reminds us daily that we live in a fallen world. In my city, stories within months of each other included an officer strangling his vibrant spouse with a barbell to maintain his affair, and morbid pedophilic actions by an elderly dentist—who had taken the young disenfranchised girl to church for years. Nonetheless, many people in most towns still herald humankind as basically good. That is, left to our own devices we will figure things out. They also contend that respect and tolerance will develop unabated.

Can you say "Enlightenment?" Or, "War to end all wars?" The latter was simply a precursor to World War II, Vietnam, Korea, Kuwait, Iraq, Afghanistan and many dozens of others—and Korean bombs will likely fly anew. We are indeed fallen creatures. Reason detached from morality is irrationality.

Teachers need to teach morality, not hesitate to label moral actions. How can we teach citizenship without warning kids of evil? In the light of the annual parade of Fritzl-types, let alone 9/11 videos, Holocaust lessons and Stalin studies, "evil" is unavoidable. Evil is not simply a misguided religion, it's in the hearts of reprobate men and women.

A momentarily violation of innocence might be labeled as cruel. We get concerned. Rapacious acts labeled as a moral crisis. We become outraged. But sustained violations of human dignity comprise a humanitarian catastrophe. We need an institutionalized response that doesn't shy from value judgments.

St. Augustine warned that, "Charity is no substitute for justice withheld."

Fallen humans with porous moral filters trample the pages of history, but aspects of this sordid behavior have become mainstream entertainment or overlooked historical realities. The HBO series Big Love accents a warped network of screwy behavior, not unlike that of some prominent religious and civic leaders (past and present). And our human history is still being written, with a wave of innocence being trampled. In numerous countries as you read this, countless kids are stowed away in brothels and factories never able to enjoy reading, let alone laugh. It's a catastrophe. The innocent need heroic voices with values in line with those of universities like Notre Dame, Taylor, Wheaton (IL), Azusa Pacific and Indiana Wesleyan.

At a Buck Creek reunion, we chuckled about Ned the naked hitchhiker. But amidst any such gathering persists the reality of our fallen natures, and that public smiles might be masking private sins. Horrible acts. Heinous crimes. And that beneath our feet might be children crying for our help. But during our reunion, with the hog roast on the lawn and Ned being roasted inside, there wasn't a hint of sinister actions. Just evidence of hard lives. Long journeys. Good marriages mixed with broken ones. Much welcome laughter. And all the while our classmate Marvin was living his dream – on stage before his peers doing his Elvis impersonation of "Love Me Tender."

Buck Creek Wisdom #44

"Reason detached from morality is irrationality."

"Charity is no substitute for justice withheld." (St. Augustine)

"Evil is not simply a misguided religion, it's in the hearts of reprobate men and women."

Buck Creek & the Bible

I suppose the bad news is we have a propensity to be bad. "When tempted, no one should say, 'God is tempting me.' For God cannot be tempted by evil, nor does he tempt anyone; but each person is tempted when they are dragged away by their own evil desire and enticed. Then, after desire has conceived, it gives birth to sin; and sin, when it is full-grown, gives birth to death." (James 1:13-15) The good news is that through Christ we have hope to do good. "I have told you these things, so that in me you may have peace. In this world you will have trouble. But take heart! I have overcome the world." (John 16:33) "Do not be overcome by evil, but overcome evil with good." (Romans 12:21)

ABOUT the AUTHOR:

Jerry Pattengale has spoken on many of the nation's largest campuses, has founded and helped direct various national initiatives, and has numerous books, publications and unique life experiences. He serves as Executive Director of the Green Scholars' Initiative, Assistant Provost at Indiana Wesleyan University, and holds distinguished positions at Baylor University, The Sagamore Institute, Gordon-Conwell Theological Seminary and Tyndale House, Cambridge. He coined the phrase, *"The dream needs to be stronger than the struggle."*